DATE DUE

Basic
Ice Skating
Skills

Basic
Ice Skating
Skills

An Official Handbook
Prepared for the United States
Figure Skating Association

by

Robert S. Ogilvie

Professional Instructor
Ice Club of Baltimore, Inc.

J. B. LIPPINCOTT COMPANY
PHILADELPHIA/NEW YORK

ISBN-0-397-00518-0 Cloth Ed.
ISBN-0-397-00519-9 Paper Ed.

SIXTH PRINTING

Library of Congress Catalogue Card Number: 68-54414

Manufactured in the United States of America

Contents

6

Illustrations and Diagrams

Illustration

8

9

Introduction

Basic Ice Skating Skills has been written for those of you, adults as well as youngsters, who are just taking up skating and want to understand and master the fundamental skills which underlie the various branches of this sport. There is very little in print that caters exclusively to the beginner, and it is hoped that this book will help fill the gap. You will find here answers to many questions you will ask even before you set foot on the ice: questions about equipment, clothing, the age at which to start children, and many others.

But first, what type of skating are you going to learn? There are, as you may know, three main branches of skating: figure skating, ice hockey, and speed skating. We are concerned here with what is very loosely called figure skating, a term which now embraces so many different types of skill that it has become extremely misleading. For those unfamiliar with the sport the idea of figure skating may appear to be any gyrations made up of turns or curves on one foot; this was known in former days as "fancy" skating, a term which nowadays should be strictly avoided unless you wish to date yourself in the eyes of the younger generation. To others, figure skating may bring to mind wintry scenes of a frozen lake on which skaters execute fancy designs consisting of numerals, letters, or even their own names. These pictures are both inaccurate and incomplete. To set the record straight it should be made clear that figure skating is divided into the following branches:

(1) the figures themselves, which consist of certain geometrical designs traced on the ice by the skater, all based on the figure eight;

(2) free style, consisting of jumps, spins, arabesques, footwork, and other movements skated to music over the whole ice surface (this is what the public sees at an ice show, and is the part usually televised during skating championships);

(3) pair skating, which is really free style executed by two persons simultaneously, but including certain combined lifts and spins;

(4) ice dancing, consisting of a type of ballroom dancing on ice comprising certain nationally and internationally recognized dances such as waltzes, fox-trots, tangos, and many others.

As you can see, figure skating embraces far more than the term suggests at first sight.

The aim of this book is not only to teach you the skills which underlie the various branches of figure skating but, for those who wish to take the sport purely as a recreation and have no desire to pursue competitive goals, to show you various skills which are an end in themselves and a pleasure to master. If you go no further than the movements contained in Part II of this book, you will be head and shoulders above the average rink skater, and in the eyes of your friends you will appear a very competent skater indeed.

This book is designed to be used as a self-instructor; as a useful additional aid for those already taking lessons; and as a reference book for coaches involved in the Basic Test Program for beginners set up by the United States Figure Skating Association. To achieve this, the skills in each section of the book have been set out in the exact order in which they should be learned. This order is the result of long and diligent research over a period of many years by my wife and myself in the field of beginning skating. It forms a system which we have proved to be both logical and successful. There are undoubtedly other systems; every instructor worth his salt has his own ideas and methods. What you will find in the following pages happens to be ours and, most important criterion of all, the system works.

The division into chapters, each containing a relatively small number of movements, has a purpose. When you have carefully studied and practiced all the movements in one chapter, stop and review those movements until you are satisfied that you have them reasonably well under control. Then, and only then, should you go on to the next chapter. When teaching yourself, there is a tendency to become impatient with difficult movements and rush on ahead. If you are taking regular lessons you will be held in check by your teacher and also by the fact that you may not know what to practice next. When learning from a book, however, it is different. The complete schedule is spread out before you and the temptation to skip is very great. This can only result in wasted time. If you want to get the most out of this book, fight this very natural temptation and work methodically.

The most important part of this book is Part II, Fundamentals. All the movements in that section are within the grasp of all and should be thoroughly mastered. If ice dancing appeals to you or if you feel the urge to jump and spin or do some interesting footwork, go on to those sections when you have mastered sufficient fundamental skills. At certain points in Part II, you will be told when you are ready to try movements contained in the free style and dance sections. As far as the free style is concerned, you can take it or leave it as you think fit. Many adults do not feel the desire to jump or spin but can still become very strong and competent skaters without it. But don't run away with the idea that adults can't learn to jump; I have taught a number of not-so-young skaters to do the simple jumps, and these adults have thereby strengthened their skating enormously. It is largely a question of overcoming timidity, strengthening basic skills, being prepared to take a few falls, and skating regularly enough to keep your balance at a high pitch.

How long does it take to master the movements contained in this book? This is difficult to answer as there are many varying factors involved (see the chapter on Preliminary Questions). However, a rough estimate would be that an average skater of reasonable talent, skating on good equipment, with access to uncrowded ice sessions and skating every week two or three sessions of two hours each, could learn fairly well all those movements presented in Parts II and IV ("Fundamentals" and "Basic Dance Movements") in nine months. A young skater of talent could do it in six months. These estimates assume, of course, that the skater has never set foot on ice before—a skater who has had some previous experience of plain skating around a rink could do it in considerably less time. As far as the free style is concerned, for a young skater to master these movements might well require another three months.

A great incentive to anyone learning a sport is to be able to measure how well he is doing. For many years the United States Figure Skating Association (USFSA) has conducted tests for its members in the various branches of figure skating. However, even the lowest of these tests required a season or more to pass. Now the Association has made available, not only to its members, but to the public at large, a series of tests starting at the very lowest levels (the first Beginner's Test only requires you to skate forward and stop successfully). Find out whether these tests are given at your local rink and apply to take them as you see fit. There are not a lot of formalities involved and you do not even have to be a member of the USFSA to take these tests. If you pass any of them successfully, you will get a lot of satisfaction and some very attractive badges for your efforts. Information on the Basic Test Program may be obtained by writing to:

> The United States Figure Skating Association
> 178 Tremont Street
> Boston, Massachusetts 02111

As your interest in skating grows, you may find it worthwhile to join an ice skating club if there happens to be one in your locality. At the time of writing there are well over two hundred ice skating clubs in this country, all affiliated with the USFSA. A few of these clubs own their own rinks, but most rent ice from public rinks so that they can hold their own sessions, during which times can be set aside for the uninterrupted practice of the various branches of skating mentioned above. Beginners are welcome, and club programs very often include group instruction at all levels. Information about location of clubs and the various test programs can be obtained by writing to the USFSA at the address given above. Among its many activities, the USFSA publishes an interesting monthly magazine, *Skating,* and an official rulebook containing, among other things, descriptions of all the official dances at present recognized in this country. It is from this rulebook that the diagrams and descriptions of the dances at the end of the section on Basic Dance Movements have been taken.

14   Acknowledgments

The author and the United States Figure Skating Association are deeply indebted to the following skaters, who gave many hours of their time to pose for the photographs used to illustrate this book: Robin Ward, Robin Williams, and Nancy Strahan from the Ice Club of Baltimore; Don Bachlott, Jr., and Renée Parker of The Skating Club of Wilmington; and Roberta Chadd of the Washington Figure Skating Club. Miss Chadd was coached by Jerry Renaud, Mr. Bachlott by Philip Fraser. The photography was greatly facilitated by the generous provision of ice time by The Skating Club of Wilmington.

In justice to the skaters who so willingly modeled for our photographs, the reader is forewarned that the "wrong" positions, although very accurate, were especially posed!

➤ *Note*: Important skating terms are defined or explained in the text, generally the first time they occur. Such words are italicized, and these special explanations are also indicated by an arrowhead in the margin like the one above (the marginal arrowhead is also used for certain other important explanations found in this book). Most key terms are defined briefly in the Glossary, with page references to the text for more detailed explanations.

1. Preliminary Questions

Parents who wish to start their children skating and adults about to take up the sport all tend to ask the same questions. This chapter deals with some of the more common ones.

Am I too old to start?

A famous dance studio used to advertise, "If you can walk you can dance," and much the same applies to skating. We have had several pupils, both men and women, who did not start until their sixties; after about a season and a half they could not only skate competently around the rink but had mastered some of the simpler dances. Younger skaters will attain relatively higher goals. So much depends on your own confidence.

Is it safe?

Skating is surprisingly safe, largely because the slipperiness of the ice absorbs much of the force of a fall. Some day you will have a fall—in fact, you will have many of them—and the sooner you get your first fall over with, the better. It is a cliché to say that the most dangerous place is the home, but it is certainly true when comparing a home to an ice rink. A fall on the rink cannot be compared to a fall down a flight of icy stone steps outside your house. You may collect a few bruises when skating, but anything more serious than this is no more likely on the ice rink than in most other sports. In fact, few sports are as safe.

How long will it take my child to learn?

What instructor has not been asked this question! Yet there is no immediate answer. How long does it take to learn the piano? It depends on what you mean by learn. When the question is put like this, most parents answer vaguely, "Well, to skate nicely around the rink." Putting aside the fact that it is unlikely that a skater will want to stop learning at this point, let us say that it depends on the physical aptitude of the child, the type of equipment used, the amount of time that can be given to practice, the quality of the instruction, and the desire on the part of the child. The right type of equipment is so important that a whole chapter will be devoted to it (see pp. 20–32).

At what age should a child be started?

There is no hard and fast rule about the age at which to start. Once a child can walk firmly, he can start at almost any age. Our own son started at the age of two, and because he had good equipment he was soon skating happily by himself. There are, however, several points to be noted regarding such an early start. Tiny children need someone with them most of the time, and if you cannot do it yourself, the constant supervision of a professional instructor can be expensive. Small children tend to ignore rink rules, such as skating in the same direction as everybody else, and are likely suddenly to take it into their heads to skate at right angles to the general line of direction, which may result in their getting knocked over or wrapping themselves around some other skater's feet. However, if someone can be with them and you have access to some fairly empty rink sessions, this objection can be overcome. As far as instruction is concerned, a tiny child may soon learn to skate confidently around the rink, but his span of attention is generally short, and it is unusual for a small child to show the desire and the concentration necessary to learn a good technique. Points that may take a couple of seasons to drive home at the age of four may often be picked up within a week or so two or three years later. Children should be put onto the ice at a very early age only if a real desire to skate is shown; otherwise they may take a dislike to the sport. There is the danger that, just when you think it is time for them really to learn something and you are arranging for them to take lessons, the novelty is suddenly found to have worn off and all interest has been lost.

17

Speaking very generally, girls tend to absorb instruction and coordinate earlier than boys. Let us say that a reasonable age to start a girl is about six years old and a boy somewhat later, at about seven or eight. But bear in mind that individual circumstances play a big part.

Should I buy my own skates?

The answer is a definite "yes" if you propose to skate regularly. At nearly all rinks you can rent skates, which may be a good idea for the first few times, but if you are interested in making quick progress, buy your own. For a detailed explanation as to why, see the chapter on equipment, starting on page 20.

What about lessons?

Take lessons by all means. They can be of untold assistance in clearing up difficulties, reinforcing what you will learn in this book, and keeping you to a schedule that will ensure steady progress. At most rinks both group and private instruction are available; which you take will probably be decided by your own budget. It is a good idea to start children off in a class, as it makes them self-reliant more quickly, but this is not necessarily so with adults. For beginners, class lessons are usually very suitable, but after a time the members of a class tend to differentiate in skill and then it is as well to consider private instruction. It is quite obvious that one's own particular problems are taken care of better in a private lesson, and certainly an adult will feel less self-conscious. Many rinks feature adult classes; housewives' groups are extremely popular and are usually held on weekday mornings for those fortunate enough to have the time. They are great fun, and these groups usually make excellent progress from the beginner stage. Men would, of course, be very welcome in these classes but few can spare the time on a weekday morning. Class lessons are much less hard on the pocket than private lessons, but if you have passed out of the beginner stage, or if you have a child who shows aptitude for the sport, private lessons become increasingly necessary.

At the time of writing, fees charged for private lessons by professional instructors of good qualifications and experience vary from $5 to $10 per half hour according to reputation, part of the country, and time of year (rates at specialized summer skating schools tend to be higher than those prevalent during the winter). However, it would be safe to say that the services of an excellent professional instructor can be obtained for an average price of $6 per half hour. Occasionally such an instructor is willing to give lessons of a shorter period based on the same rate. However, policies of rinks and instructors vary somewhat in this. Many rinks employ junior professionals who do give fifteen- or twenty- minute lessons at a slightly cheaper rate.

In choosing a professional, bear in mind that the best qualification a teacher can have is that of teaching successfully. Most rinks will allow spectators into the rink at a nominal fee, and you can usually get a good idea of the reputation of an instructor by casual conversation with other skaters or the rink management.

Prices of group lessons in public rinks vary enormously, depending on such factors as whether the price of admission to the rink on the day of the class, or extra practice sessions, is included in the total fee. A typical example might well be $25 per group of ten weekly half-hour classes, admission to the rink included. How long these rates will last with inflation at its present level is difficult to say.

If you are an adult and rather timid, you might enjoy the added confidence provided by an instructor when you first step onto the ice. Most adults, if the equipment is reasonable, and with the help of an instructor, can take a few walking steps unaided at the end of half an hour. They won't be skating properly but they can usually progress forward. With children and more confident adults there is no harm in trying alone for the first few sessions. Keep the rail within reach and try to get the feel of the ice and the skates. As soon as you have some semblance of balance, arrange for some lessons or read the section on Beginning Stroking, in Chapter 3, starting on page 33, which will tell you how a correct skating thrust is made. Don't leave it too long before you start thinking about the thrust or you may develop bad habits that are difficult to eradicate. The correct movement is not one you are likely to hit upon naturally; it has to be learned.

Whether you have frequent or infrequent lessons, the important thing is to take them regularly. The fact that you have another lesson scheduled for a definite time ahead tends to make you try harder to master what you have already been shown so as to have it ready for the next lesson. The number of lessons you take depends on how often you skate, how keen you are to get on, and your pocketbook. It is not necessary to have a lesson every time you skate. In fact, it is very important to have practice time between lessons. Which brings us to the next question.

How often should I skate?

To make good steady progress you should be on the ice a minimum of two or three times a week. Many skaters make progress on a weekly two-and-a-half-hour practice session, but it is slow going and most of their time is spent in getting their balance back to where it was when they left off the previous week. It is not so much a question of learning but of maintaining the feeling of balance. The average session at a public rink lasts two and a half hours, but three short practice periods of, say, forty-five minutes each during the week will be far more beneficial than one long one of two and a half hours at a stretch.

2. Equipment

In the United States, the word "skate" is usually taken to mean the combination of boot and blade, but strictly speaking the *skate* is the blade. There are four different types of skate: figure, hockey, racing, and children's double runners. We are concerned here only with figure skates. Even if the eventual aim is to play hockey exclusively, the basic skills should be learned on figure skates. One good reason is that the hockey blade is much higher than the figure blade and thus encourages the natural tendency of the ankle to drop inward. This is made worse by the fact that the hockey boot is lower than the figure boot and therefore gives less support to the ankle.

Children's double runners are fine if you just want your child to trot around the rink with you, but he will learn just as much walking around the living room floor in his shoes, which would be cheaper anyway, and he may resent being put onto single blades later on. Double runners do not glide satisfactorily. It is quite impossible to teach a child even the rudiments of skating on them. We have no hesitation in condemning them strongly.

It will soon become apparent that you cannot skate forward around the rink with both feet glued to the ice; between thrusts you have to be on one foot, and you cannot skate on one foot unless your ankle is erect. Therefore your boot must be constructed of a good, firm leather and be of a sufficiently snug fit so that, with a correctly placed blade, it will hold your ankle vertical. The blade should be of a good steel so that it will glide properly and hold an edge when sharpened.

These are the minimum requirements of a pair of skates, and when so stated they seem pretty obvious. We are constantly astounded at some of the junk people tie on their feet and on which they optimistically hope to skate. We see boots several sizes too large; boots devoid of arch supports; boots made of leather having the strength and consistency of thin, floppy kid gloves; boots with no heel (common in the cheapest children's boots); blades so blunt that they will slide as easily sideways as forward; blades so rusty that they will not slide in any direction—equipment, in fact, that can only make a mockery of any attempt at skating. I think my own feelings about so-called bargain skates are best summed up in the words of John Ruskin: "There is hardly anything in the world that some man cannot make a little worse and sell a little cheaper, and the people that consider price only are this man's lawful prey."

The natural reaction of someone new to skating is to buy the cheapest equipment in sight. The usual excuses are, "I thought these would be good enough to learn on," or, "I thought I'd see if I liked it first." How can you like skating if you are walking around the rink on the sides of your ankles! And you certainly cannot learn anything. In the case of a child it is invariably, "But she is growing so fast, she'll be out of them in no time." The last complaint is a valid one, but there are ways around the problem. Some skate shops, particularly if run by a rink, will offer a reduction, sometimes quite large, on your second pair of skates if you trade in the first within a specified time and if they have been kept in reasonable condition. Your first pair is then offered for resale. The fact that children grow out of boots so quickly means that it is often possible to pick up a good used pair that has had comparatively little use. Within a large family, skates can sometimes be handed down. For the first few sessions you can also rent skates, and some rinks have very good rental equipment, but such skates usually suffer very hard wear.

For reasons that I hope are now becoming clear, buying boots a size too large in the hope that your child will grow into them is throwing money down the drain, especially if you are spending money on lessons at the same time. The child cannot learn anything because the boots don't fit, and by the time they do fit the boots are so distorted and worn out that they are no good anyway. Face the fact: if the equipment is below standard it will be impossible to learn anything worthwhile on it, and if you cannot learn anything you probably won't enjoy skating.

You don't have to go out and get the most expensive equipment money can buy. There is, however, a price below which the equipment ceases to do the job it is meant to. Probably one of the best sources of information is the professional instructor at your local rink. Ask him what is the most reasonably priced equipment that will do a good job. Make friends with some of the people who skate regularly and find out what they are using and whether they are satisfied. Relatively few firms in the United States specialize in making skating boots and blades, and their equipment is usually sold through rink shops and a few of the better sporting goods stores. One advantage of purchasing through the rink shop is that they know that if they sell you poor or ill-fitting skates and you go to the rink pro for lessons, he is not going to be pleased. There is nothing more frustrating for an instructor than to have a pupil on inadequate equipment.

Digest everything in this chapter before rushing off to the local rink; it will help you discuss matters as though you know what you are talking about.

The boot

You are looking for a boot of good-quality leather that will not lose all support after a couple of months' use. You are also looking for a boot of the right size. This is vital, because if the boot does not fit, the quality of the leather is wasted. To do a good job the fit must be very snug, especially around the ankle. When the boot is laced properly, there should not be a lot of up and down movement of the heel inside the boot. Hold the heel of the boot firmly down with your hand and see if you can lift your heel away from the bottom of the boot. If you can do so to any great degree, the heel may be too large. When you bend your knees there should not be too much buckling of the leather around the ankles. It is not always possible to get everything perfect in a stock boot, but the less movement of the heel and the less buckling of the leather, the better. Nowadays it is customary for girls to wear white boots and boys black.

Contrary to what most people think, the average skater takes a half size smaller than his walking shoe and not a half or whole size larger. Naturally the larger boot feels more comfortable, but this does not mean it fits well. With a true fit there is bound to be some discomfort at first because of the snugness and solidity of the leather. A good boot needs several sessions of breaking in before it molds to the foot. There are exceptions to the half-size-smaller rule, of course. The person with a very broad foot, say a D, may have to have a boot a little too long so as to get sufficient width. However, within reason, this does not matter provided the heel fits well. If you are prepared to pay a little extra you can get one of the better makes of stock boot, which come in fittings ranging from triple A to E, although your dealer may have to send to the factory for the more unusual widths.

Now look at Illustration 1, which shows the various parts of a skating

23

Skating Boot and Blade

Illustration 1

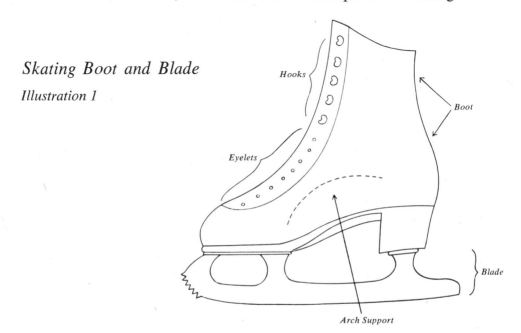

Hooks

Boot

Eyelets

Blade

Arch Support

➤ boot. All the better boots have a built-in arch support, or *counter,* as it is sometimes called, either of very strong leather or steel. It is unwise to buy a boot without one. The lacing gap should be wide and the tongue well lined.

Have your boots fitted while wearing a pair of socks of normal thickness (nylon socks are quite satisfactory) or Danskin tights. Do not wear several layers of thick woolen socks; they take away from the support of the boot and do not keep the feet any warmer because you have to lace more tightly to get proper support and this impedes circulation. You will find the remedy for cold feet dealt with under the heading of Clothing.

24

The blade

Illustration 2 shows a modern figure blade from the side and from below. You are looking for a good steel, first because it will have good gliding qualities over the ice and second because some of the poorer quality blades cannot be sharpened properly.

The ugly-looking spikes at the front of the blade are known as the
➤ *toe picks* or *toe rakes* and, although they tend to scare beginners at first, they are put there for a purpose. Their primary use is in certain spins, jumps, and other movements met with in *freestyle* (see Introduction). Also, although a correct thrust is made from the side of the blade and not the toe, the toe picks can be of assistance to the beginner in that when the thrusting foot (i.e., the one being left behind) is turned out correctly, the lowest pick leaves the ice last and prevents the blade from slipping sideways. If you trip over them, it is almost invariably because the foot is being returned incorrectly after the thrust (see Illustration 10C, p. 44). If the lowest toe picks are very sharp, you

The Blade Illustration 2

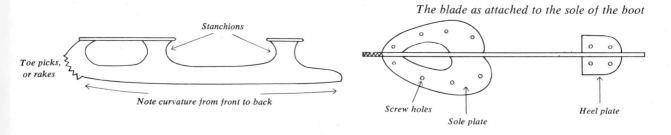

The blade as attached to the sole of the boot

Toe picks, or rakes

Stanchions

Note curvature from front to back

Screw holes

Sole plate

Heel plate

may have them blunted just a little, but make sure the grinder knows he is not to take them off completely. Once they're gone, they're gone, and you may regret it later. Here again, the local professional will be able to give you the best advice.

Many people are ignorant of the fact that there must be a hollow running the length of the bottom of the blade (Illustration 3A). This creates two distinct edges to the blade: an *inside edge* and an *outside* ◄ *edge*. If this hollow is absent, the blade will tend to skid sideways across the ice, not only preventing the skater from thrusting properly but also giving him a great sense of insecurity. *Grinding,* or *sharpening* (the terms are used synonymously in most rinks), consists not only in sharpening the two edges of the blade but also in restoring the hollow, which tends to flatten out with use. The depth of the hollow, too, plays an important part—just any old hollow won't do. If it is too shallow, the blade may skid and will certainly lose its edge quickly, while if it is too deep the blade will sink too far into the ice and thus become unmanageable as well as slow running. On the average ice, the blade will run well if the curvature of the hollow corresponds to that of a silver dollar, or perhaps a little deeper. For an advanced figure skater the hollows are much more critical and varied. It is best to have a competent grinder at the local rink sharpen your skates. The local hardware store does not always understand the necessity for a proper hollow and smooth finish, so that your blade is apt to present the appearance shown in Illustration 3B, a blade that has been cross ground and not smoothed out properly afterward. A bad grinder can ruin a pair of blades in no time at all, so if you find a competent man, value him as you would a good doctor. It may cost more at the rink than at the local store, but it is usually worth it.

How often should your blades be sharpened? It is impossible to give

25

Construction of the Blade   *Illustration 3*

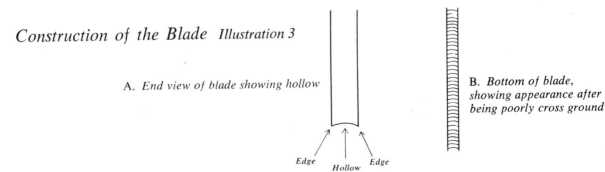

A. *End view of blade showing hollow*

Edge   Hollow   Edge

B. *Bottom of blade, showing appearance after being poorly cross ground*

a hard and fast answer to this very common question. So much depends on how often you skate, how heavy you are, the quality of the blade, how deep a hollow you are using, and how careful you are off the ice. As a rough indication, I, who spend six days a week on the ice, sharpen my skates about once every three weeks, but I know adults skating only once a week who go through a whole six-month season on one sharpening.

Note that a figure blade is curved from front to back. This curve is known as the *radius,* or *rocker,* and the greater part of this curve is normally part of a circle having a radius of approximately six feet. It is this curve that is one of the main differences between a figure blade and racing or hockey blades, which for the greater part of their lengths are straight, although some skaters have their hockey blades ground with a very slight curve. (Hockey and racing blades are also much thinner than figure blades.)

26 ➤

The quality of a blade can often be assessed by the quality of the weld where the vertical section of the blade joins the sole and heel plates. This weld should be smooth and almost undetectable.

Setting the blade

➤ *Setting the blade* means placing the blade in the correct position on the sole of the boot. You can buy your skates as a *matched set* (boots with blades already attached by the factory), or you can buy boots and blades separately and have the dealer attach the blades to the boots for you (this is technically termed "mounting" the blade). Because most firms in the skating business specialize in making either boots or blades but seldom both, the best equipment is bought separately, the blades then being positioned on the boots and screwed on. You notice I said *screwed* on. If you look at the majority of the cheaper matched sets, you will see that the blades have been riveted on at the factory. This might be all right if the blade were riveted in the right place, but it seldom is. Here and now I should like to say that there are several firms in the business whose matched sets are a good buy, with the blade correctly set, but if you intend to buy a matched set, do get some advice on it first, preferably from the local professional.

How often do we see some poor beginner struggling around the ice with his ankles dropped over to the inside and sometimes practically walking on the sides of his boots! Most people think that this happens because they have weak ankles, but unless there is an actual deformity this is just not so. The fault lies either in a boot that is too large or lacking in support, or in the setting of the blade, the position in which the blade is fixed on the boot. The blade should not be set down the center of the boot but somewhat to the inside of the midline. This helps to offset the natural tendency of most people's ankles to drop in, or "pronate." Illustration 4 should make this clear. This is the reason it is better to have blades that are screwed on and not riveted. You may find that your physical structure calls for a more inside setting than normal, in which case it is relatively simple to unscrew the blade, have the screw holes properly plugged, and reset the blade. In the case of very young children this often has to be done. Even with a correct setting there has to be some slight attempt by the skater to develop the habit of keeping the ankle erect. A correct setting makes this possible while an incorrect one makes it almost impossible. Sometimes young children will not make even this slight effort, and a very exaggerated

27

Blade Setting

Illustration 4

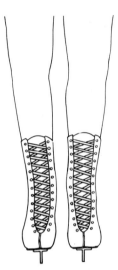
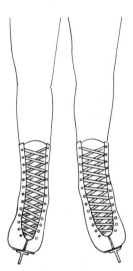

A. *Blades correctly set to the inside of the midline of the boot*

B. *Blades incorrectly set to the outside of the midline of the boot, causing the skater's ankles to bend*

inside setting is necessary. As they get older this setting can gradually be corrected to a normal one.

Watch out for the very cheap matched set in which the boot has a plastic sole. The blades are invariably riveted on, and even if you succeed in detaching the blade with a hacksaw it is almost impossible to screw it back on again! Plastic soles are satisfactory, however, if the blade is set correctly.

Don't be surprised if your skates are returned to you after setting with only three screws in the front and a couple at the back. This is so that you can test the setting; in case it should need altering there are still screw holes that can be used. When you are satisfied with the setting, you can have more screws put in, but it is not really necessary to have all the screws put in, and it gives you some latitude in case you decide to alter the setting later on.

Lacing

A boot will not feel as though it fits unless it is laced properly. Laces should not be too thick; if you can get them, the nylon ones are best, particularly if they have a slight give to them. Do not lace too tightly around the toes or at the top. When the boot is laced properly, it should not be possible to get a finger under the laces (except at the top of the boot). In Illustration 5, note the area where the lacing should be tightest. To get proper tightness it may be helpful at first to use a small hook,

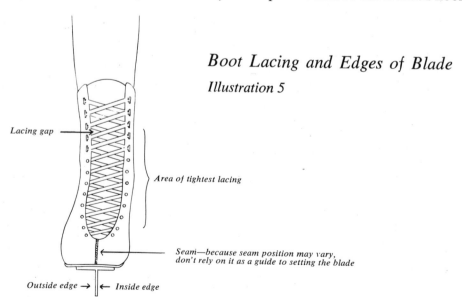

Boot Lacing and Edges of Blade

Illustration 5

Lacing gap

Area of tightest lacing

Seam—*because seam position may vary, don't rely on it as a guide to setting the blade*

Outside edge → ← Inside edge

but with practice this can be dispensed with. Parents, please teach your children to lace their own boots at the earliest possible age. Most children are much more capable of this chore than they will admit. If they cannot do up their boots and a lace comes loose when you are not available, they are stuck.

Care of equipment

Most skate shops sell lacquers for the soles and preparations for the uppers that are designed to keep your boots watertight, but boots do not necessarily deteriorate without their use, provided you remove excess moisture after skating and keep them in a dry atmosphere.

Always dry your blades after use, and when walking around off the ice use skate guards. It is amazing how many skaters fail to realize the dreadful damage they do to their blades by stepping on metal and concrete without guards. I have even known children to walk home on their unprotected blades! Unless there is a rubber matting or some other suitable soft flooring round the rink and leading to the ice from the dressing room, guards are essential. These can be purchased at the skate shop and are made out of rubber, plastic, or wood.

The better wooden guards have the advantage that the blade is supported at both ends and the cutting edge remains clear, and also that they usually make a clicking sound when you walk, thus making you more conscious that you are wearing them. This reduces the possibility of your charging out onto the ice without taking them off. When this happens, the clattering fall that results is one of the most spectacular in skating and, provided you are not hurt, one that is usually greeted by gales of laughter, especially if it is done by the professional. If you are unfortunate enough to do this, keep your head. The first instinct is to try to rise to one's feet and retire to the side in a dignified manner, but the process simply repeats itself. Just sit there and remove your guards before you do anything else. You will feel an awful fool, but take comfort from the fact that almost every skater, even a champion, does it at least once if not several times during his career. In

29

fact, I did it three Wednesday afternoons in a row until I think my pupils began to accept it as my usual mode of entry onto the ice surface. (By the way, don't put your skates away with the guards on, as this encourages rusting. Your guards should only be used for walking around off the ice.) See, too, that your name is written indelibly on them; this will save a lot of confusion and may also prevent their loss.

Constantly check the tightness of the screws holding the blade to the boot, particularly when your boots are new. Two to three days after a blade has been attached to a boot it is possible to give the screws at least an extra half turn. Failure to do this may result in moisture penetrating the screw hole, causing rust, which in turn results in the screw losing its thread. Always carry a screwdriver in your skate case as a piece of standard equipment. (Incidentally, most skaters carry their equipment to and from the rink in the type of bag used by airlines, but specially shaped skate carriers are also available through certain suppliers. Ask for information at the skate shop of your local rink.)

One last tip: if the metal tip of a nylon lace is lost, simply soften the end of the lace in a match flame and after a couple of seconds roll the end into a point. It will set immediately and be as good as the original tip, if not better.

Custom-made boots

Most top-rank skaters have their boots custom made in order to ensure the closest fit possible and therefore the maximum control over the blade. The average skater with a fairly normal foot can nearly always get an excellent fit in one of the better stock boots. There are occasions, however, when a person has an unusually shaped foot—for example, wide in front with an extremely narrow heel. If your foot is of this type you may have to consider having a boot made for you if you intend to pursue your skating. The success of such a boot depends partly on the ability of the person who takes the measurements and partly on how closely the maker follows them. The local professional probably has his boots custom made, so ask his advice. The rink shop may be com-

30

petent to undertake the measurements, but it is more likely that you will have to visit the firm itself or some accredited supplier.

Clothing

For girls, and ladies as well, the usual skating outfit consists of suntan Danskin tights, a short skating skirt (often pleated) with brief skating pants to match the skirt, a blouse, cardigan or sweater, and underclothing as necessary according to the temperature of the rink. Gloves are optional. Boots should be white and kept clean. Note that we say the pants should match the skirt; there is a tendency not to do this nowadays, but it is advisable unless you want to focus attention on your rear, which very few ladies wish to do. Mothers, please note that it is not the custom on the ice rink to wear tights alone, as is often the case in the ballet studio. A girl should always wear brief skating pants in addition to her tights and skirt. And no long scarves, please! They are a menace on the ice.

31

If your rink is very cold, you may disregard these rules and wear just about anything you please. There is no point in being miserable, so in the depths of winter get yourself a pair of warm slacks and as many sweaters as you need. As instructors we have to spend many hours standing on the ice and have found the various types of insulated underwear invaluable. Don't put up with cold feet, either. It is no good stuffing your boots with extra socks, as this simply impedes circulation because of the tighter lacing necessary. The only real cure is proper boot covers, worn over the boot. A pattern is shown in Diagram 1.

Boot Cover Diagram 1

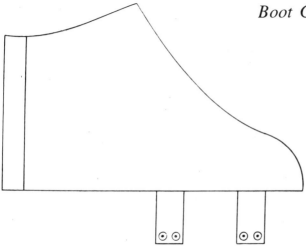

The boot cover is constructed of two halves of thick blanket wool. The two halves are sewn together along the front side only. A half inch must be allowed for this seam and for the hem around the bottom of the cover. At the back is a band of Velcro which will overlap a matching piece on the other half of the cover when put on the boot. Two pieces of one-and-one-half-inch elastic with press studs are sewn on one half, as shown. The matching studs will be sewn on the other half on the outside of the hem.

They should be of fairly heavy white blanket wool. Many skaters try to use white socks with the bottoms slit open but, while these give the impression of a nice clean boot without the trouble of having to clean them, the material is just not heavy enough to keep the feet warm. Although the feet may still feel a little chilly, the difference in comfort with boot covers when the temperature is around freezing is quite remarkable. They may not look particularly neat, but a skater just cannot concentrate on what he is doing when suffering from frozen feet.

32

For the boys' and men's clothing, just about anything goes. At one time men were dressy creatures on the ice, but that is all past now, which is rather a pity. There is not much choice nowadays, and the main thing is comfort: slacks, sweater, gloves optional; hats should not be worn by males in closed rinks. The boots should, of course, be black.

In many rinks, local clubs rent the ice in order to practice various branches of skating, including ice dancing. If you become expert enough to take part in the dance periods, you will have lady partners, in which case a jacket is indispensable. Please do not turn up without one, even in the hottest weather. It is most uncomfortable for a girl to have to dance with a partner whose shirt is clammy and sticking to his back.

Part II

Fundamentals

3. First Objectives

First time on the ice

You are standing at the side of the rink plucking up your courage to step onto the ice for the first time. Don't be put off by the fact that the other skaters all look as though they have been at it for years. Skaters are entirely concerned with their own affairs and are so used to seeing beginners around the side of the rink that they scarcely even notice them.

Your boots are laced properly and you have taken off your guards, which you have put in some accessible place near the entrance to the ice surface.

We will assume that you are unaided. Take a good grip on the rail or barrier and step carefully onto the ice. Your first reaction may well be that you have never felt anything so slippery in your life, but rest assured that this feeling will soon wear off. At this point there is no doubt that a professional instructor can be of great assistance. It is scarcely practical to hold this book in one hand and the barrier with the other. However, if you are reasonably athletic and have confidence in yourself, it is quite possible to manage without physical aid. Beware of the helping hand of a friend unless you are sure he is rock steady himself. There is a skill in holding and assisting a beginner that only comes with considerable practice and experience. Not only that, it is no good leaning on someone and having him carry you bodily around the rink. Balance is a combination of feel and confidence. It is something that requires conscious effort on your part to learn.

Now, collect your feet, bring them together underneath you, and try to stand still. You may slide your feet back and forth several times just to get the feel of things. However, your main objective right now is to move forward without holding on to the barrier. At this stage don't worry about too many details. Take no notice of your friends at the side telling you to bend your knees, push with the blade, and so on— first things first, and the first requirement is to get some degree of balance while you are actually moving. Your instinct is to take walking steps, which you will soon learn is not correct, but just while you are getting the feel of the ice this does not matter too much, provided you make the steps small. If at this stage you really lack confidence in yourself and cannot bring yourself to get away from the rail, you will find that a good instructor can usually get even the most timid beginner moving forward cautiously but unaided at the end of about half an hour, provided reasonably good equipment is being used.

34

A. *After a fall . . .*

Right way

Getting Up from a Fall

Illustration 6

B. *roll over . . .*

C. *onto one knee . . .*

D. *get one foot underneath you . . .*

Just as soon as you have sufficient balance to glide forward a little way on two feet, you can start to learn the elements of the correct stroke, but there is another vital subject to be discussed first.

Falls

Falls on the ice are not nearly as bad as those on the floor or ground This is because you slide when you hit the ice and much of the force is thereby absorbed. You will often be told that as soon as you feel yourself falling you should bend your knees and try to relax. This is all very well in theory, but a beginner usually finds himself sitting on the ice without having had the time to do what is necessary on the way down. You will eventually learn to relax, but, really, you can only learn to fall by falling and, although this may sound rather brutal, the sooner you have your first fall and get it over, the better. The fact that you find it did not hurt as much as you expected and that you are still in one piece adds immeasurably to your confidence.

35

When you fall, get up as quickly as you can. Don't just lie there. All you do is attract attention, and other skaters (particularly the pro, who is usually busy giving a lesson) feel impelled to come over and check to see whether you are all right. In Illustration 6 you are shown the right and the wrong way to get up from a fall. Apart from any other consideration, the wrong way is exceedingly inelegant.

Beginning stroking

Stroking is the action of propelling oneself across the ice by means of a correct thrust from the side of the blade combined with correct

Wrong way

E. *then the other, and you're back in business*

F. *If you try to get up like this . . .*

G. *you'll end up like this!*

timing of the rise and fall of the skating knee, correct timing of the transference of weight from one foot to the other, and neat footwork. It is a far more subtle movement than many skaters, even experts, realize. Stroking requires constant revision and practice even after you have been skating for a considerable time. In this chapter we cannot go into the subject too deeply, because to stroke well requires that you balance on one foot for a considerable distance, and you have only just learned to glide forward a very short distance on two feet. However, you can make a start to get the action.

The movement of stroking is a gliding one, first on one foot and then the other. The subject will be dealt with much more fully in Chapter 4, but at the moment the main thing is to realize that you should get your push from the side of the blade and not the toe. Look ahead at Illustration 9, pages 42–43. Stand with your feet close and parallel as in A, bend your knees, and turn your right foot out as in B. Keeping the whole of your right blade in contact with the ice, push against the ice with it as in C and try to glide a short distance on the left foot (D and E). You will not go far on that foot and you will have to bring your right foot smartly up to the left foot again as in F and G. This is because you have not yet learned to skate properly on one foot (this is dealt with in the next chapter), but at least it will prevent your falling into the very bad habit of pushing with the toe picks.

Having made your first thrust and brought your feet together again as in Illustration 9G, you should now glide a little way on two feet. Try to keep your arms and shoulders square to the direction of travel. You will probably find that after the first push your shoulders tend to rotate. Wait until you have your shoulders reasonably under control again, then turn your left foot out and repeat the process. As you bring your feet together you will find that you automatically tend to straighten both knees, so don't forget to bend them again before each push. Note that you should start the knee bend before and not during the push. As you push, first with one foot and then the other, say to yourself, "Push, together, pause . . . push, together, pause . . ." and so on. During the pause both feet should be on the ice. This helps you to recover your balance from the previous push and you will find that with practice the pause between the pushes will become shorter and shorter. Don't worry about the skaters behind you—they can see you and, anyway, you are not yet in a state to take evasive action.

Before we go any further, let us be clear which is the pushing or thrusting foot. It is a surprising thing that most beginners firmly believe that the pushing foot is the one they are about to push forward, whereas in fact the pushing foot is the one that actually does the thrusting and gives the power. In Illustration 9 (B through E) it is the *right* foot that is the pushing foot. In the same illustration note also that the head stays over the left foot. The whole body moves as one piece—one foot is not thrust forward ahead of the body as in walking. Later on you will discover that most of the time you will be skating on either one foot or the other. This requires that at all times there must be one foot directly under your center of gravity, which in plain forward skating means that it will be directly under your head. You will learn more about stroking after you have mastered the exercise at the beginning of the next chapter. The main things to bear in mind just now are that the knees should start to bend before the stroke, the push should be made from the blade and not the toe pick, and the back should remain straight throughout. Fight the temptation to bend forward at the waist as you bend your knees.

Stopping

At this point it is usual to introduce the beginner to the simplest stop, the snowplow. It will serve its purpose for the moment, but it is strictly a beginner's stop and should be abandoned as soon as you have learned one of the other methods.

Get up a little speed and then glide forward on two feet, allowing them to run parallel to each other, about eighteen inches apart. Bend both knees strongly, lean slightly back and turn your toes in, still preserving the distance between your feet (Illustration 7, A and B). If you succeed in holding your feet in this position, you should skid

A. *Bend your knees and turn your toes in*

B. *Side view; note slight backward lean*

C. *One-foot snowplow. Some find it easier*

slowly to a stop. It needs quite a bit of power from your thigh muscles to keep your feet where they should be, and it helps to think of the movement as one of pushing both feet out to the side and away from each other. Also, the ankles must be dropped over slightly to the inside or else the blades will not skid. However, if you drop them over too much, the edges of the blade will catch, and, again, the blades won't skid—you must experiment to find the correct angle. Certainly, if you do the reverse, as many beginners do—that is drop the ankles over to the outside—your feet will immediately run together and you are liable to pitch forward. It is essential to keep the weight back, as in 7B, when making this stop. (Many skaters find it easier to use one foot only. Start in the same way as for the two-footed method but then turn the body slightly sideways and use the leading foot to make the skid, as in Illustration 7C.)

4. You Learn to Stroke

Skating forward on one foot

It is now time to learn to place your weight centrally over your blade so that you can skate firmly in a straight line without veering off to one side or the other. You must master this exercise before continuing your study of stroking.

Get up a little speed and glide forward on both feet, keeping them as close as possible (Illustration 8A). The head and shoulders should be erect, back muscles firm, hands and arms extended to the side and very slightly in advance of the body, weight distributed evenly on both feet, and knees slightly flexed. Carefully ease the weight over onto the right foot, still keeping the left foot in contact with the ice (8B). Note how the skater's head is now centered over her right foot. Here comes the tricky part. As soon as you feel you have nearly the whole of your weight over the right foot, allow your left foot to come gently off the ice and pass back until it is about a skate's length behind the right foot (8C). Do not push with your left foot as you allow it to come off the ice. This is very important: don't push with the foot that you are taking off the ice; just allow it to take up its position in back. If you push as the left foot comes off the ice, you are apt to drop the whole of your left side and your right foot will probably turn out, with the result that you will no longer be centered over your skate and the whole object of the exercise is lost. As your left foot comes off the ice, try to continue on your right foot in as straight a line as possible.

(Now is a good time to point out that the foot on which you are actually skating is known as the *skating foot* while the foot that is in the air is called the *free foot*. If you are skating on the right foot, every part of the body on the right side bears the term "skating" before it— *skating leg, skating knee, skating hip, skating shoulder,* and *skating arm*—while every part of the body connected with the foot in the air— in this case the left foot—bears the word "free" before it—*free leg, free arm.*)

40

The first few times they try this exercise, beginners are almost invariably plagued by one thing: they cannot keep the blade running in a straight line. If they are on the right foot they veer to the left and if on

Forward Gliding on One Foot   Illustration 8

A. *Weight evenly distributed on both feet*

B. *Place your weight over the skating foot*

C. *Allow the free foot to take up a position behind*

D. *Wrong: weight not centered over skating foot*

E. *Wrong: skating ankle dropped over onto inside edge*

Errors

the left foot they veer to the right. This is because either the weight is not over the skating foot (8D), probably because both feet were never brought together properly as in 8A when starting the exercise; or because the skating ankle is dropped over to the inside (8E). Either of these faults will rock the blade over onto its inside edge, causing it to run in a curve. You will learn to use these edges to get curves in Chapter 7, but just now they are a nuisance. If you want your blade to run in a straight line, it must be erect so that both edges of the blade bear an equal weight; otherwise, if the blade is dropped over to the left, it will curve to the left, and vice versa. The natural tendency is for the blade to drop to the inside, so you can now see why it was stressed in the chapter on equipment that the blade must be correctly set on the boot to offset this.

41

A tendency to curve away from the straight line may also be caused by allowing the free hip to swing back as the free foot is taken off the ice. Keep your hips nearly square to your direction of travel and firmly under control during the exercise. Another common fault is to attempt to balance from the waist or with the free leg. In fact, many years ago the free leg was actually called the "balance leg." However, skating has progressed since then and, although in certain movements the free leg does assist the balance, there is no doubt that the main factor in control of balance is the skating knee, which functions rather like the front wheel of a bicycle. If you remain firm at the waist and maintain a firm free leg, your blade will have a much better run over the ice. Remember, however, that the skating knee is almost never held in a rigid locked position; even when rising fully on the skating leg, the skating knee remains very slightly bent.

A question that is commonly asked is, "What part of the blade should I be skating on?" Because the blade is curved from front to back (see Illustration 2, p. 24), you only skate on one small portion at a time. The actual part of the blade used varies a little with different makes, but generally speaking when skating forward you should be skating toward the back of the blade and when skating backward more on the middle to front section. If, at a later stage, you cannot seem to get on a part of the blade that seems comfortable, consult your local professional;

it may be that your blade is too short for the boot or has too strong a curve from front to back, or that persistently bad grinding has caused it to curve away too strongly toward the heel.

The above exercise should, of course, be practiced on the left foot also. Try to attain sufficient balance so that you can stay on one foot and hold a straight line for a distance of at least twelve feet. Avoid becoming "one footed." Remember the skater's well-worn adage, "double practice on the weak foot."

42

Essentials of stroking

Now that you can skate on one foot, both right and left, we will study the basic stroke in more detail. As a preliminary exercise you should stand still with your feet together, your back straight, head erect—in just the position, in fact, that was just described for skating forward on two feet. Now bend both knees, keeping your back absolutely straight as you do so. The natural tendency is to bend the top part of your body forward as you bend your knees, and this must be overcome. Rise up again and repeat the process until you have learned not to stick out at the back with every knee bend.

Now look again at Illustration 9.

A. Stand square to the direction in which you want to go, head and shoulders erect, knees slightly flexed, arms slightly to the side so that your hands are about at hip level.

B. Bend both knees and turn the right foot out so that the whole of the blade is in contact with the ice.

Correct Stroking 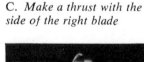 Illustration 9

A. *Stand still with feet together and back straight*

B. *Turn right foot out and start to bend both knees*

C. *Make a thrust with the side of the right blade*

D. *End of thrust, left knee fully bent, head over skating foot*

C. Thrust firmly against the ice with the right blade without allowing it to slip.

D. Glide forward on the left foot, continuing the knee bend.

E. The right foot has now left the ice with the toe pointed out and down. It is important that there should be no thrust from the toe at this point. All the power has already been gained in the action shown in C and D.

F. The right foot is now being returned. As soon as the return action is started, rise evenly on the left leg.

G. As the feet come together again, start to bend both knees before . . .

H. Making the new thrust with the left leg.

There are several points worthy of note in Illustration 9, one of the most important being that the push from a standstill, or from rest, as it is termed, is different from that used when already in motion. In B, C, and D, the push from rest with the right foot is made directly back, while, once the skater is in motion, the push from the left foot (9H) is made slightly to the side, after which every push, both from the right and left foot, is made slightly to the side. Note that, whatever the pushing foot is doing, the foot on which you are skating travels more or less directly forward and not to one side and then the other. (In actual figures, such as the "eights" p. 164, the sideways thrust is not used even when in motion, but you should use it in general skating around the rink.)

The way in which the foot is returned from the position shown in 9E is very important. The knee of the free leg (the one in the air) bends

E. *Thrusting foot leaves ice, toe pointed down and out*

F. *Thrusting foot returning; skating knee straightens*

G. *Feet together again; both knees start to bend for next stroke*

H. *Skater now moving so next thrust is made with sideways action*

very little. This is made possible by the fact that during the return of the free leg the knee of the skating leg rises evenly, thus allowing room for the returning leg to come up to the other one without catching the toe pick of the returning foot on the ice. Also, during the return, the blade is kept parallel to the ice surface and the foot turns in gradually and evenly during its travel until it is brought close beside and parallel to the skating foot (9F and G). Compare the way in which the foot is being returned in Illustration 10C. Here, the toe has been turned down toward the ice instead of being kept parallel to the ice surface, causing the toe pick to catch in the ice, resulting in the stumble seen in 10D. This is one of the commonest causes of falls by skaters who are unused to figure skates. Instead of having the toe picks ground off, learn to return your foot properly.

44

Illustration 10A shows a correct stroke being made, while 10B shows the obvious errors of leaning forward and deliberately thrusting with the toe pick. Please look again at Illustration 9, C, D, and E, and note once more how the body moves forward as a unit, with the head remaining all the time over the skating foot. One of the most important axioms for a beginner to bear in mind is that there must always be at least one foot under his center of gravity.

When you have mastered the movements just described, there is still the problem of obtaining maximum power from the thrusts while preserving a smooth and apparently effortless action. A powerful thrust can be obtained only by keeping the weight of the body over the skate

Errors in Stroking   Illustration 10

A. *Correct stroke from side of blade; back straight, head up*　　B. *Wrong: pushing from toe pick and leaning forward*　　C. *Wrong: foot returned with toe pointed down . . .*

that is doing the thrusting. To make this clear, stand for a moment with both feet together and turn the right foot out. Put nearly all your weight on the right foot, and you will find that it is possible to make a firm thrust with it onto the left. Now stand as before and put nearly all your weight onto the left foot. The thrust that you can now make from your right foot will be very weak indeed. You can thus see that it depends upon which foot bears the weight of the body whether the thrust is powerful or not. It is not too difficult to get a good thrust from a standstill because you have time to get your weight placed correctly before you start. The problem comes when you are in motion. A moving thrust requires a certain time and distance to execute, and during this time and distance the weight has to be transferred evenly from the thrusting foot to the new skating foot.

45

Diagram 2 shows the typical marks left by the blade on clean ice when a skater starts from a standstill and strokes smoothly and powerfully up the rink. It will be seen that the lines are not of even thickness. This is because the more weight there is on a blade, the heavier will be the mark on the ice. At the bottom of the diagram the skater is standing still, about to move up the rink; the right foot is turned out and bears nearly all the weight of the body. The initial thrust is made from the right blade, which makes a mark on the ice similar to that at point A. The skater is now moving straight up the rink on the left foot. At B the feet have been brought together, but because the weight is still on the left foot, the mark made by the right blade at this point is scarcely

Correct Stroking

Diagram 2

*Typical marks left on clean ice
when stroking correctly*

D. *resulting in a fall through
catching toe pick in ice*

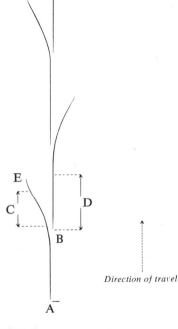

Direction of travel

visible. At this same point the left foot is allowed to turn out at about the angle shown and, still bearing nearly all the weight of the body, makes a thrust in the region marked C. During this thrust the feet get farther and farther apart and the weight is gradually transferred onto the right foot, as is shown by the gradual thickening of the line in the region marked D. Note how the line at E becomes fainter as the weight is finally shifted to the new skating foot. At this point your left leg will be fully extended and, if you have succeeded in making your thrust as described and have timed your knee bend as shown in Illustration 9, your thrusting foot will leave the ice softly and take up a position with the toe slightly turned out and a few inches above the ice surface. This is possible because the main power of the stroke has been obtained at C and not at the end of the stroke. If the stroke is mistimed and the weight transferred too soon onto the new skating foot, the thrusting foot will tend to kick up at the end of the stroke in an ugly, jerky fashion.

To achieve the correct timing of the transfer of weight from one foot to the other requires an enormous amount of practice, and at this stage you may, at best, make only a passable attempt at it. Stroking has been treated here at some length because it is the foundation of all skating. It may be several seasons before your stroke fully matures, and you must work at it constantly. You should start every practice session by stroking for at least five minutes without stopping, making sure that you use a full rise and fall of the skating leg. Gradually increase this time to ten minutes without stopping. Although the strength in the leg muscles that this stroking exercise develops is indispensable, the real value lies in the rhythmic rise and fall that it teaches. This rhythm cannot be over-emphasized: it runs through all skating. The difference in jumping ability between two young skaters of otherwise equal proficiency one of whom has stroked regularly and one of whom has not, is quite unbelievable. The rhythmic skater has learned to feel instinctively when he must relax and when to exert power.

Stroking style and technique differ somewhat among top-rank free-style skaters, many of whom adopt a slightly rolling stroke that makes more use of the inside edge. However, the technique described in this chapter is the fundamental one on which all stroking is based.

(Before leaving the subject, I should mention that when you come to ice dancing and the consecutive forward edges dealt with in Chapter 9, requirements of edge techniques, appearance, and, in the case of ice dancing, simply to avoid kicking your partner will make it necessary to turn your thrusting foot out to a greater degree and make a more backward thrust than called for when generally stroking around the rink. In fact, when skating figures, as was mentioned earlier in this chapter, the moving thrust is almost identical to that made from rest.)

47

Skating backward

You can and should learn to skate backward just as soon as you have learned to skate forward, in fact, the earlier the better. This is particularly so in the case of adults, whose skating progress is likely to be abruptly terminated by their inability to skate backward, due, usually, to sheer timidity.

There are two distinct methods generally in use to teach a beginner to go backward; some instructors favor one method, some the other. Both methods involve *two-footed movements* (both feet remain on the ice during the movement). Later on, you will learn to skate backward on one foot, but not right now. The principle of the backward stroke is entirely different from that used when skating forward.

First Method. This is undoubtedly the more difficult method of the two, but if you can get the hang of it, it has the advantage that the movement prepares you for, and more nearly resembles, the advanced backward skating movements on one foot that you will learn later on. Illustration 11 shows the movement. Stand as in A with your feet about a skate's length apart. Keeping your arms and shoulders square, move both heels to the right by a twisting movement from the waist (11B). By another twist from the waist, switch your heels now to the left and then to the right again and continue the movement, trying as you do so to move backward. In all probability on your first few tries you won't move off the spot, but with a little perseverance and luck you will get the knack of it and away you go. However, if you really can't seem to make any headway, here is a more detailed analysis of the movement

A. *Start: feet apart and knees slightly bent*

B. *Switch heels to right; weight over right foot*

C. *Switch heels to left, transferring weight to left foot*

D. *Turn heels again to right and repeat movement*

48

E. *Wrong: weight moved too soon to left foot; compare with B*

Backward Skating: First Method

Illustration 11

that may be of use to you. During the switching of the feet from side to side there is a very tricky little rock of the body weight also from side to side, and it is the mistiming of this rock in relation to the switching of the feet that prevents you from moving backward. When both heels are to the right, most of the body weight should be over the right foot (11B). During the switching of the heels to the left, the weight of the body is transferred to the left so that it settles over the left foot just as the switch is completed. This causes a semicircular cut in the ice with the inside edge of your right blade and creates a thrust which should start you moving. If you switch your weight away from your right foot too early or too quickly (as in 11E), there is no pressure from your right blade and consequently no backward movement. The reverse is, of course, true when you switch your feet from the left to the right. To get the feel of the movement it often helps to stand as in 11A, then, turning your toes slightly in, rock from side to side, lifting

A. *Start: turn both heels out*

B. *Feet separate, skater moves backward*

C. *Continue movement by drawing feet together*

D. *Feet together again; restart movement without pause*

Backward Skating: Second Method   Illustration 12

49

first one foot and then the other off the ice. While doing this, start the twisting action again and you will probably get the feeling of the movement.

Second Method. This is by far the easier and more quickly learned method of getting moving backward. It is, however, not so good technically as the first method, and a glance at Illustration 12 shows that it offends against the principle of having one foot under your center of gravity at all times.

This time start with your feet fairly close and turn your toes in as in 12A, bending your knees as you do so. Allow your feet to separate as in 12B, at the same time pressing on the inside edges of your blades. As your feet spread apart you will move backward. When your feet have separated as far as you dare let them go, draw them in again (C) until they are together as in D, at which point you will repeat the process. The backward movement should be a continuous one, without any pause when the feet come together. This progression across the ice by moving both feet in and out is known as *sculling*. Sculling, incidentally, can be done forward as well as backward and is often used by the girls in ice shows who appear to move across the ice without any visible means of propulsion when they wear voluminous period costumes that hide their feet.

As soon as you have mastered either of the two methods and can move backward at a reasonable speed, bring both feet together as close as your balance will allow and practice gliding backward on two feet in a straight line. This will prepare you for the next exercise.

5. A Turn and a Curve on Two Feet

Turning from forward to backward

Provided you can now glide backward on two feet in a straight line with your feet kept fairly close together and parallel to each other, you can go on to this next exercise, which is to turn from forward to backward while in movement. Here again, as in learning to skate backward, there are two distinct methods, one much simpler than the other. Both are two-footed movements and will be superseded at a later stage by more advanced methods.

50 *Turn from Forward to Backward: First Method*
Illustration 13

A. *Skate forward, turn head and shoulders to right and . . .*

B. *turn backward (skater traveling toward camera)*

C. *Wrong: curving to right as shoulders turn to right. Compare with A.*

First Method. Skate forward with both feet fairly close together; now turn your head and shoulders strongly as in Illustration 13A. It is essential at this point that your feet not turn with your shoulders and that you continue to skate in a straight line. Exert a little more pressure with the shoulders, switch the lower half of your body quickly around, and you will be skating backward (13B). Illustration 13, D, E, and F, shows the same movement viewed from the side. This method is an uncomplicated one and very suitable for young children. The most common error is for the skater to allow himself to make a curve as he thinks of turning his shoulders (13C), resulting in his coming to a dead stop. The position in 13A is a difficult one to hold but is the key to the whole turn.

Second Method. This is a much prettier and more advanced way of turning from forward to backward; Illustration 14, A through D, shows the movement from the side.

Start by gliding forward on two feet, keeping them parallel and about half a skate's length apart. Now let the right foot come slightly forward, still in contact with the ice, as in 14A. At this point, shift most of your weight onto the left foot and turn your right foot out, keeping the forepart of the blade in contact with the ice. This will start you turning to the right. When you are halfway around the turn, as in 14B, switch your left foot around so that it is parallel to the right foot as in C, at the same time drawing the right foot back and level with the left. If you have done everything correctly you should be skating backward along the same straight line on which you started (14D).

51

Turn viewed from side

D. *Skater traveling forward, across camera*

E. *Head and shoulders turn, but feet not yet. Same position as A.*

F. *Turn made, skater is now traveling backward*

If you find that your right foot resolutely refuses to turn out, it is simply because you have too much weight on it. However, you must keep the right foot lightly in contact with the ice or it won't turn you at all. Also see to it that your left foot continues on in as straight a line as possible while you make the first part of the turn. If it curves across your line of travel too much, you will come to a dead stop. Learn this movement in both directions.

52   Forward curve on two feet

Up till now, you have done all your skating on a straight line, but you are soon going to discover that most skating consists of curves, or ➤ *edges,* as they are technically called. The following exercise prepares you for learning curves on one foot, which you will do in Chapter 7.

Get up a little speed forward, bringing your feet as close together as possible with your shoulders and arms square to your direction of travel. Now lean to the left and you will find that because of the construction of your blade you will make a curve to the left (Illustration 15A). At first you will probably do what the skater is doing in 15B, and that is to keep your feet too far apart and not really lean, but it is not a difficult movement and you will probably succeed in making the curve after two or three tries.

The important thing is to lean all in one piece and keep your feet

Turn from Forward to Backward: Second Method
Illustration 14

A. *Just before turn; most of weight on left foot*

B. *Turn right foot out, but left foot continues forward until . . .*

C. *turn is made by switching left foot around, parallel to right*

D. *Draw feet level with each other to complete turn*

close together. Note in 15A how the skater is leaning from the blade upward—the ankles follow the line of the lean and are not held erect as some skaters think. Don't get your weight too far forward on your blades or you may skid. Now try the same movement to the right until you can do it equally well either way. At first your curves will be quite shallow, but with a little practice you should be able to make curves that are part of a circle having a diameter of about three times your height.

Unless there are very few people on the rink you will have to practice this, and many of the movements to come, in the center of the ice surface. In most rinks it is the custom to reserve the center ice for skaters practicing movements that do not take them around with the general flow of traffic, which most of the time is counterclockwise.

53

When practicing these curves, you may find that your circle tends to get smaller and smaller and that you get into a slow spin. If this happens don't fight it; just bend your knees, let your feet go apart, and allow yourself to come to a stop.

Skating backward on one foot

This next exercise is of vital importance. It consists of learning to glide backward on one foot (on both the right and the left foot) in a straight line for a distance of at least three times your own height. Practice this constantly while you are working at the movements in Chapters 6 and 7. You will need to have mastered it before you can attempt any movements in Chapter 8, so this should give you plenty of time.

A. *Correct: note how body leans in one piece from ankles up*

B. *Wrong: feet too far apart, causing a lean away from curve*

Forward Curve on Two Feet

Illustration 15

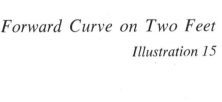

Get up a little speed backward, with your feet as close as you can get them and your arms and shoulders square to your line of travel, as in Illustration 16A. The skater in this illustration is, of course, moving away from the camera. Now get your weight onto the right foot as in 16B and carefully allow your free foot to leave the ice to take up a position directly behind the right foot, preferably with the toe turned out and down as in 16C. Note that you learn this in exactly the same way you learned to skate forward on one foot; if you turn back to Illustration 8C (p. 40), you will see the similarity.

54

At your first attempts you will find the exercise remarkably difficult to execute. At this stage it is probable that you just won't be able to bring yourself to get the left foot off the ice at all; this is caused by

Skating Backward on One Foot *Illustration 16*

A. *Skate backward with weight evenly over both feet*

B. *Shift weight over one foot*

C. *Allow other foot to take up a position behind*

D. *Wrong: weight not centered over skating foot*

E. *Wrong: ankle dropping over to inside*

Errors

failure to get sufficient weight over onto the right foot or, in the case of adults, sheer timidity.

When you finally succeed in getting one foot off the ice, you will find that you curve off to one side. This is caused sometimes by failure to center oneself over the skating foot as in 16D or by allowing the ankle to drop over as in 16E. It is a strange thing that, while you may have mastered keeping your ankle upright when skating forward, the old habit reappears as soon as you start to skate backward on one foot. At this stage most beginners are unaware that they are dropping the ankle of the skating foot over to the inside. It helps to have a friend watch you do it and tell you if and when you get your ankle upright.

You may also find that at your first attempts you tend to pitch forward and rise up on the toe pick of your skating foot. Again this is due to fear caused by unfamiliarity with the balancing action when traveling backward. However, with a little perseverance you will master the balance.

You should, of course, practice this exercise equally on the left foot. The real problem is that at this stage you are not sufficiently in control to turn your head, and therefore cannot see who is behind you. It is a good idea to have someone skate forward in front of you to warn you if you are likely to run into anyone. Don't, however, allow him to touch or hold you.

A frequent question is, "Why can't I do it with my foot in front?" The answer to this is, first, that, in the case of a beginner, it tends to pitch the body weight backward so that you may catch your heel in the ice and, second, the position with the foot behind is better practice for the movements you will learn in Chapter 8.

6. Basic Stops
and Terminology

The T stop

You should now be ready to abandon the snowplow stop in favor of the T stop, which is much more efficient. It is just as well to learn this stop both on the right and the left foot, but most skaters, even advanced ones, tend to stick to one foot almost exclusively.

First, get up some speed forward in a straight line on one foot, with your head and shoulders square to your direction of travel. Let us assume that you are skating on the left foot. Now bring your right foot up to the left in a complete T position, holding the right blade parallel to the ice surface but not yet touching it. Lower your right blade very gently to the ice, at the same time turning your right ankle slightly over onto the outside edge, as in Illustration 17B. Provided you can hold this position with your feet at right angles to each other and also that the blade is lowered onto the ice in the way shown, you should gently skid to a stop. Front and side views of the stop are shown in 17A and B. Note in 17A how the skater keeps her head, shoulders, and arms absolutely square to the direction of travel.

Errors. The most common error in the T stop is to put the foot down with the ankle dropped over so that the inside instead of the outside edge of the blade touches the ice. If you do this, the blade will scrape

56

instead of skidding, causing you to swing around off the straight line. Stopping with the front part of the blade instead of the middle will have the same effect. These two faults are shown in 17D and 17E.

Another fault is to put too much weight onto the back foot before you are used to the feel of the stop. You must learn to do it gently at first, and then you will gradually find that you are able to put more and more weight onto the back foot until you can lift the front off the ice, as in 17C. The skater in this photograph is very expert and is shown executing the stop at considerable speed. It will be a long time before you can do this, but it is good to have a picture in your mind of what you are eventually aiming at.

57

T Stop   *Illustration 17*

A. *Shoulders and blade at right angles to direction of travel*

B. *Side view: note angle of ankle, pressing blade onto outside edge*

C. *Advanced form of T stop. Only for experts!*

E. *Wrong: stop made by dragging toe pick, shoulders rotating*

D. *Wrong: ankle dragging on inside edge of blade*

Errors

Fundamentals

One other common error is to fail to put your back foot onto the ice at a complete right angle to the skating foot; this results in your feet separating and no skid is possible. When the stop is done correctly, a small shower of snow will be thrown up behind the skidding blade. If, instead, you find that you have collected a small pile of snow in front of your back blade, you are not putting your blade onto the ice at the correct angle.

There is another type of T stop in which the skidding blade is put down at right angles in front of the skating foot, but this is not for beginners and is used mainly in exhibition skating when a pretty-looking stop is required.

58

A. *Correct: shoulders facing line of travel. Note position of feet.*

Hockey Stop
Illustration 18

Getting the feel of the stop at the barrier

B. *Wrong: right foot has passed across left; head and shoulders rotating*

C. *Skate toward the barrier at a slight angle*

D. *Put both hands on barrier and skid with both feet— see text*

The hockey stop

As its name implies, this is a favorite of hockey players and is the most efficient stop of all. However, it is usually used only when traveling fast and in an emergency.

Skate forward, again with your arms, head, and shoulders square to your line of travel, but this time allow your feet to separate so that they are just under a skate's length apart. Then, still keeping your head and shoulders firmly in position, suddenly throw both heels to your right, leaning back and bending your knees strongly as you do so, as in Illustration 18A. Both blades should have been switched immediately to a position at right angles across your line of travel and, properly executed, you should skid to a stop in a remarkably short distance.

Although not requiring any great degree of skill, this stop is not an easy one to learn because you cannot do it by halves; you must do it completely or not at all. If you do not turn your blades at a full right angle across your line of travel in one quick movement all you do is go off on a curve to one side. Try learning it at the boards (Illustration 18, C and D). Skate toward the boards at a slight angle as shown in C; then, when you are really close, put both hands on the boards and turn your heels out (D). You must be close or you will reach too far forward with your hands, so that your feet just curve into the boards instead of skidding. The only thing about this way of learning to stop is that it does not allow you to keep your head and shoulders square to your line of travel, but it does give you the feeling of what happens to your feet.

Apart from allowing the shoulders to swing out of position, a common error is to allow one foot to swing across in front of the other. If you are turning your heels to the right, the right foot is the one that gets out of position, as in 18B. Because of the rotation set up, this error can cause a twisting fall, so be careful. Think of it this way: if you are traveling with your feet parallel to each other, each foot turns at right angles on its own line of travel. Before trying the stop you can practice the turning-out movement while standing still.

59

Two Back Stops
Illustration 19

A. *Back toe scratch. Lean forward when stopping this way.*

B. *Back T stop. A superior method but tricky.*

60

Backward stopping

The two most usual ways of stopping when skating backward are shown in Illustration 19, A and B. In the first method, skate backward with your feet fairly close, then slide one foot behind you, at the same time leaning forward. Now carefully raise the back heel until the toe picks of that foot lightly scrape the ice, bringing you to a stop. It is not difficult to do, provided you remember to slide one foot behind first. It is no good skating backward with your feet level and just trying to scrape the toe: all you will do is to fall over backward. This may sound stupid, but you would be surprised how many people try to do it that way even after it has been demonstrated correctly.

Far better but much more difficult is the back T stop. Skate backward on, let us say, the left foot, with your shoulders square and the right foot directly in line behind and at right angles to your line of travel. Now bend your left knee, lean forward, stretch your right foot well back, place it lightly on the ice on the inner edge, and you should skid to a stop. At first you will misjudge the amount of weight to be put on the skidding foot, but a little practice will put this right.

There is another way of stopping when going backward that resembles the forward snowplow. You skate backward with both feet well apart, turn your toes out and push slightly outward at the same time. Both blades will skid and bring you to a stop. You can also use the method of rising up on both toes, but although you will often see it done it is not recommended.

Free Side and Skating Side
Illustration 20

Skating side | *Free side*

Terminology

Here we shall review and examine in more detail some of those terms with which you are already slightly familiar, and, because skating terminology unfortunately has never been 100 percent standardized, introduce you, where necessary, to some of the alternative terms that you will often hear used among good skaters and meet in skating literature.

The word "edge" is used in two slightly different senses. It can mean one of the two actual physical cutting edges of the blade, or it can mean the curve made when you lean to one side and only one of these edges is cutting into the ice. In this sense the skater uses "edge" as a synonym for "curve." As you can be traveling *forward* or *backward,* ◄ and at the same time be on either an *inside* or an *outside edge,* you can see that each blade can make four different curves and therefore in this sense possesses four edges. Thus we speak of a "right forward outside," "left back inside," and so forth. In writing, these terms would be abbreviated to RFO and LBI respectively. So, if you see RBO in print you will know that you should be on the *r*ight foot, skating *b*ackward, and leaning over onto an *o*utside edge. When the meaning is clear, the word "edge" is frequently omitted: thus, a "left forward outside" means a left forward outside *edge.* Also, in the United States, the words "outer" and "inner" are often used instead of "outside" and "inside."

You have already had some experience of the effect of forward edges when you made curves on two feet. In the next chapter you will start to tackle edges on one foot in earnest. This means that you will have to use shoulder, arm, and leg positions that are more elaborate than those you have used up till now, so you must understand exactly how these positions are described.

In Illustration 20 the skater is skating on the right foot; therefore everything on the right side of the body bears the word "skating" before it (skating hip, skating arm, skating leg), while all parts of the body on the left side bear the word "free" in front of them (free leg, free shoulder, etc.). This has already been mentioned at the beginning of Chapter 4. Occasionally the terms *employed* and *unemployed* are used in this sense instead of *skating* and *free*. Thus you may hear a skater refer to the employed hip instead of the skating hip. "Employed" and "unemployed" are considered rather old-fashioned now, but they are still sometimes used.

➤ The skating foot is occasionally referred to as the *tracing foot*. This is because, on clean ice, the blade leaves a white line which is called, when one is actually skating figures, the *tracing,* or *trace.* Even when not skating figures, skaters will often use the term to mean the general line of travel, and it is common to hear such phrases as "Keep your free foot over the tracing," which means that you should hold your foot either behind you over the line you have just made or over the line you are about to make. A good skater knows by the context which is meant.

Another source of confusion is "forward" and "back" and, of course, the alternative terms "in front," "in back," and "behind." When skating forward it is pretty clear; if you are told to put your foot forward, or in front, you know where it should go. But if you are skating backward, where is "in front"? Should you think of it in relation to your body or your direction of travel? Actually, it means exactly the same place as if you were skating forward; you should think of the position in relation to your body, *not* your direction of travel.

➤ *If you are athletically inclined, your balance should now be good enough for you to try the movements contained in the first chapter on Basic Free Style, Chapter 13.*

62

7. Key Positions; Forward Edges and Crossovers

Four key positions

We shall now make use of what you have just learned to describe the four most important combinations of arm, shoulder, and leg positions. Note that, generally speaking, when an arm is forward the corresponding shoulder is also forward, and when an arm is back the corresponding shoulder almost invariably is also back.

Let us assume that the skater is moving forward. The position in Illustration 21A is described by saying that she has her skating arm forward and her free arm and free leg back. Now look at the picture immediately below (21E). Here the skater is moving backward with the arms and free leg in exactly the same position. But the description is the same: she still has her skating arm forward, and her free arm and free leg are still described as being back. Look at the remaining pictures in the top row. In B the skating arm and free foot are forward while the free arm is back. In C the free arm is forward and the free leg and skating arm are back. In D the free arm and free leg are both forward while the skating arm is back. The pictures immediately below show exactly the same position as far as arms and free legs are concerned and therefore the description is the same, even although the

A. *Skating arm and shoulder forward, free leg and free arm back*

B. *Skating arm and shoulder forward, free leg forward, free arm back*

C. *Skating arm and shoulder back, free leg back, free arm forward*

D. *Skating arm and shoulder back, free leg and free arm forward*

E.

F.

G.

H.

Same positions as A, B, C, and D but with head turned

skater is now traveling backward. The difference between the two sets of positions is that of the head, which also can be described as looking forward or back irrespective of direction of travel.

Incidentally, in these two sets of illustrations, don't be misled by the head positions. For the sake of putting the point across we have said that the skater in the top row is skating forward and in the bottom row skating backward, but don't always assume when looking at a skating photograph that a skater is of necessity skating in the direction he is looking. Illustration 21, A through D, could just as easily be of a skater traveling backward.

When the skater is in a position square to the line of travel with neither arm definitely forward, as in 21I, the arms and shoulders can
➤ be described as in a *neutral position,* which is the position you have always used up till now. The positions shown here are the most funda-

Four Key Positions of Arms,
Shoulders, and Free Leg

Illustration 21

I. *Arms and shoulders in*
"neutral"

mental ones in skating. However, to avoid the criticism that these have been oversimplified, it should be mentioned that there are many subtleties that you will learn later on, particularly in regard to hip positions, which will be dealt with in Chapter 8.

Study these key positions at home until you are absolutely sure of them, so that if you are told to put your free arm forward you can do so immediately without having to think about it. By the way, if you are skating on one foot and you are told to put your foot back, please don't ask, "Which one?" That is the sort of question that makes instructors leave skating and take up insurance.

The forward outside edge

You will now learn the forward outside edge, in three stages. Nearly all the movements in this book are described either on one foot or the other but, unless told otherwise, you should practice them equally on both feet or, in the case of two-footed movements, in both directions.

First Stage. Start with a curve on two feet to the right as you did in Chapter 5, but this time your right arm and shoulder will be held forward and your left arm and shoulder back, as in Illustration 22A. Your shoulders will be at an angle of about 45 degrees to the line of the curve you are making, your right hand will be over the line you are about to make, and your left arm and hand will follow the line of your shoulders and remain outside the curve. Get as much weight as you can over the right foot and, without pushing, allow your left foot to leave the ice and take up a position about a skate's length behind your right foot. If your left foot is turned out correctly, the instep should be directly over the tracing (remember, this is another name for the line of the curve you are making). Carry your hands a little below waist level with the palms facing the ice surface and the fingers closed. Your weight should be toward the back of the blade; 22B and 22C show the position from the front and side. (Head and eyes should be looking a little more in the direction of travel than shown in the illustration.)

The first thing you will notice when you finally succeed in getting onto the edge is the difficulty of holding your position. Your body will want to turn in the direction of the curve. If, as is the case here, you are traveling in a clockwise direction, your body will tend to rotate in a clockwise direction. This is shown clearly in 22D. The whole of the body is swinging around, causing the free leg to pass outside the curve; the skating arm is now inside the curve and the free arm has come forward. The first position is totally and irretrievably lost. This uncontrolled rotation is known as *swing* and is the skater's worst enemy. It is of the utmost importance that you try to maintain the first position, as shown in 22B and C. However, it will take considerable practice before you can hold it for any great distance. At first the curve you make will be quite shallow, probably forming part of a circle having a diameter of twenty to twenty-five feet, but you should try to reduce this to a curve having a diameter of about three times your own height. When you can do this and hold your position for about a third of a circle with no swing you will be doing well. Eventually a slight rotation will start and only a very expert skater can eliminate it entirely. When you think you have the edge reasonably under control, look down at your skating hand after you have gone a few feet. It is still over your

66

Learning a Forward Outside Edge   *Illustration 22*

A. *Make a curve on two feet, weight on right foot*

B. *Allow left foot to take up a position behind*

C. *Right forward outside edge, side view*

line of travel? This is one of the easiest ways of telling whether you are getting out of position. Remember, however, to think of your arms and shoulders as one solid piece. By sheer willpower you might keep your hand over the curve but still let your shoulders swing out of position.

How do you prevent swing on this particular edge? Even when you think you are holding everything firmly in position, you may still find you are getting out of control. If you really are holding your arms, shoulders, and free leg correctly, the trouble can usually be traced to the free hip; the minutest forward movement of that hip can start a rotation that may not be felt for some distance but remorselessly increases until your position is completely lost. It is usually possible to see or sense what your arms and legs are doing, but it is very difficult to tell whether your hips are doing something they shouldn't. Your free hip can creep forward even though it is attached to your free leg, which you are holding resolutely back. Therefore, at the moment of starting the edge you must put a firm backward pressure on the free hip to lock it into position. What this all boils down to is the fact that at the beginning of the edge no part of your body should move except the free leg, which is taking up its position behind.

67

Swing has been discussed at some length because it occurs on all edges. On every edge the principle of holding your position until you have brought it under control holds good. We have referred to the starting position on the forward outside edge as the *first position*. Each ◄ edge has a first position that gives maximum control immediately after the start, and most authorities in the skating world agree on these

Errors

D. *Wrong: free foot swinging outside curve, shoulders rotating*

E. *Wrong: "hipping" (skating with hip pressed into circle)*

F. *Wrong: weight too far forward on blade, causing skidding*

G. *Wrong: skating ankle held too erect*

starting positions. There is general agreement, too, on the other positions, but there have been several systems of numbering them. Apart, therefore, from the first position, with which you will be expected to be thoroughly familiar, all other positions will be described and not numbered.

How long it takes to learn the forward outside edge depends a great deal on your own confidence. However, if after persistent attempts you are still having difficulty, it may be that your blade is set too far to the outside of your boot; such a setting can make the outside edge considerably more difficult to learn.

Probably the most common error is failure to lean in one piece, causing the skating hip to stick out, as in 22E. This is known as *hipping* and is a bad fault that will cause difficulties later on. If you are aware of it, however, it is easy to cure by simply keeping your skating hip firmly in.

Skaters often find that, when first learning the outside edge, their blade tends to skid. Provided that your blades are ground correctly (p. 25), the cause is almost invariably that your weight is too far forward on the blade. This fault is being demonstrated in 22F. Try getting your weight farther back.

Skating with the ankle too erect (22G) is another error. It may be your fault or it may be the blade setting. Check with an expert.

Some readers may wonder why the forward outside edge has been taught before the forward inside, which is generally considered to be the easier to learn. The reason is that at this stage many skaters still have a problem in preventing their ankles dropping slightly to the inside. Learning an outside edge tends to correct this while learning the inside edge exaggerates it.

A. *Note free foot carried slightly inside curve*

B. *Same position as A viewed from inside the curve*

Forward Inside Edge

Illustration 23

Second Stage. Get onto an outside edge and, when you feel you have it under control, bring your free foot up to your skating foot as in 22A; then, bending your knees, make a thrust directly back, finishing once more in the first position. Repeat this exercise several times on both the right and left edges. Practice at least twice as much on the weaker foot. Note that the thrust is made straight back and not to the side, as you were told to do when stroking around the rink.

Before going on, there is another expression you should know. We speak of pushing or thrusting from, but *striking* onto, a blade or edge. The strike refers to the action of setting the new skating foot onto the ice, or it can refer to the place or mark made on the ice where the strike occurs. Do not confuse the word "strike" with "stroke."

◄ **69**

Third Stage. This consists of standing still and making a strike directly onto the outside edge. It is called a *start from rest.* Turn back ◄ to Illustration 9, A through E (pp. 42–43). The start from rest is made exactly like this except that your arms and shoulders will be in the first position and you will lean over onto the edge as you thrust.

There are several points to watch for here. Assume you are striking onto a right outside edge. As you bend your knees before the thrust, you must prevent your right hip from pushing out to the right. Keep it in, and under your right shoulder. As you thrust, try to prevent your hips from rotating toward the curve you are going to make, i.e., to the right. The tendency to make both errors is very strong, and a corkscrew movement of the hips is likely to start as soon as you think of bending your knees, even before you have made the thrust. Remember, too, that the edge is made just by leaning; fight the desire to turn your head and body around in the general direction of the curve. Try to hit the edge right away and don't wander off on a long straight line before

C. *Wrong: free foot passing across curve, causing "swinging"*

D. *Wrong: failure to keep free hip and free shoulder forward*

E. *Wrong: first position exaggerated, causing rotation against curve*

Errors

you think about the lean. You must assume your lean before the thrust is completed.

The forward inside edge

We can dispose of this edge much more quickly than the outside because you are now beginning to understand the principles of skating and its language.

Assume you are going to learn the right forward inside edge. The first position is very different from that of the outside. Take a little speed and make a two-footed curve to the left. Have your shoulders square to your line of travel, with your left arm forward and somewhat inside the curve. The right arm follows the line of the shoulders and is held outside the curve. When you have the position, allow your left foot to come off the ice and take a position behind your skating foot and inside the curve. Study Illustration 23, A and B. To repeat: when skating a forward inside edge the shoulders are square (neutral), the free arm is forward inside the tracing, the free leg is back and inside the tracing, and the skating arm is to the side outside the tracing. If the back end of the blade of your free foot is just over the tracing, your free foot will be in about the right position. An important thing here is that your hips should be fairly square to your line of travel. Whatever you do, don't press the free hip back; if anything, you should think of pressing it slightly forward.

Common Errors. Once again, swing is your enemy. On the RFI (right forward inside) you will be traveling counterclockwise and your swing will generally tend to be in the same direction.

The common fault of pressing the free foot too far across the tracing is shown in 23C. This tends to pull the free hip back, and you are soon out of control. In 23D the skater has failed to hold the shoulder square to the curve, while in E she has so wildly exaggerated the shoulder position that a swing has been set up in the opposite direction. Although not so common as the other two, this error is frequently seen.

70

The key to the control of the first position on a forward inside is to keep the free hip pressing slightly forward.

Forward crossovers

Forward crossovers are also called *runs* and at a later stage are used ◄ to get up speed on a curve. Even for those of you who don't ever want to skate fast, forward crossovers are an interesting and useful exercise. They consist of a movement on a curve in which the free foot is passed around and across the skating foot. Nearly all skaters find them much easier to do to the left, or counterclockwise, but they should be practiced the other way as well.

Start on a left forward outside but this time with your free arm and shoulder forward and your skating arm back, as in Illustration 24A. Holding this position, pass your free foot in a circular movement around and in front of the toe of your skating foot until you can place it down inside and parallel to the curve on a right forward inside (24B). Now comes a very important part. As your weight goes onto the right foot, bend your right knee strongly and make a thrust with the outside edge of your left blade. The thrust is made in a direction outside the curve and not directly back. This thrust really consists of a deepening of the left outside and can only be done properly when the right knee is very strongly bent. The left foot is now lifted off the ice by a *slight straightening of the right leg* and is placed alongside the skating foot (24C); both knees start to bend again and a normal stroke is made somewhat to

Forward Crossovers Illustration 24

D. *Strike onto original left forward outside edge and repeat*

C. *Bring feet together again and prepare for new thrust*

B. *Cross right foot round in front of left onto a forward inside*

A. *Starting on a left forward outside edge*

the side as in general stroking (24D). Then repeat the action.

The foregoing is a description of how it should be done, but it will be some time before you can prevent the usual error of thrusting directly back with the toe as in 24H. A good exercise is to cross the feet as in 24B and just hold this position on both feet, traveling on an RFI and LFO. This in itself is not easy, but you will learn a lot from it. Now practice picking up the back foot, resisting all temptation to thrust directly behind.

72

The error of stepping onto a rising right knee instead of a bending one is shown in 24I, while 24J shows the ugly habit of stepping over the left foot instead of around it. During the whole crossing-over action, the free blade should be kept very low and parallel to the ice surface. As

(Illustration 24, continued from preceding page)

Forward crossovers viewed from the front

E. Skater on left forward outside edge

F. Crossover is made onto right forward inside

G. Note sideways thrust from left foot as crossover is made

you put your foot down, see that the middle of the blade touches the ice first. Don't lift your toe and put it down heel first; this gives a heavy, ugly look to the feet.

Now reverse all these instructions and try the crossovers in a clockwise direction. This time you will start on your right forward outside with your left arm and shoulder forward, pass your left foot around and in front of your right onto a left forward inside, simultaneously making a thrust from the outside edge of the right blade, bring your feet together again, and strike onto the right forward outside.

Of all the movements so far tried, skaters find this by far the hardest to execute in both directions, most having a decided preference for the counterclockwise direction.

73

H. *Wrong: pushing from toe pick*

I. *Wrong: straightening right knee as crossover is made*

J. *Wrong: stepping over instead of round the skating foot*

Errors

8. A Three Turn
and a Mohawk

In the following chapter you will learn movements requiring that you become much more conscious of what you are doing with your hips. Before proceeding, you need to be familiar with two other terms that are in common use among skaters and in skating literature.

Open and closed positions

In Chapter 6 you found that the two main positions of arms, shoulders, and free leg were either forward or back (we will ignore the neutral position for the moment). When you learned the forward edges you found that the hips also had two main positions: the free hip could be forward or it could be back. Another way of expressing this is to say that the hips are in a *closed position* when the free hip is forward and in an *open position* when the free hip is pressed back. Illustration 25A shows the closed position and 25B the open.

Of course, the thinking reader will realize that when we speak of the hips in this way, we are really speaking of a rotation of the whole pelvis. That is to say, it is impossible to push one hip forward without the other moving back at the same time. It is, however, usually more convenient to think of the hips individually.

The terms "open" and "closed" are sometimes used to refer to the position of the free leg; if it is forward, it is· in a closed position and, if back, in an open one. The arms and shoulders are also occasionally referred to in this way.

74

All the positions shown in Illustration 21 (pp. 64–65) could be done with open or closed hips. In some circumstances this might be good and in others not. Provided a skater is skating in good form, a position is correct if it assists in the proper execution of a movement, and incorrect if it does not. In many cases the hips will look after themselves, but you should be aware of the positions so that you can use them when told to do so.

Forward outside three

A *three* (also called *three turn*) is a turn on one foot from forward ◄ to backward or backward to forward, made on a curve. Diagram 3 shows what the tracing should look like if made on clean ice. The diagram also shows that the turn gets its name from its resemblance to the numeral 3. The direction of rotation is the same as that of the natural swing of the edge, which is fortunate. If you are traveling in a clockwise direction, your foot will turn in a clockwise direction, and vice versa. Because it is made on a curve, a turn started on an outside edge will end up on the inside, and if started on an inside will finish on an outside.

The three you will learn here, which is by far the most useful one at this stage, will start on the forward outside and finish on the back inside. Every three takes its name from the starting edge, so this will be called a forward outside three.

How will you be able to learn this if you have not yet learned a back inside edge? That will be no problem provided you can skate firmly backward on one foot as you were taught to do in Chapter 5. If you still haven't mastered this, go back and practice it and do not attempt anything further in this book until you have. As for the back

A. *Free hip pressing forward: the hips are "closed"*

B. *Free hip pressing back: the hips are "open"*

Open and Closed Hip Positions

Illustration 25

A. *Preparing for the turn on the right forward outside edge*

B. *Skating foot three quarters of way around the turn*

C. *Coming out of turn on an RBI; position strongly checked*

D. *Front view of A. Note free foot held back while shoulders turn.*

Forward Outside Three

Illustration 26

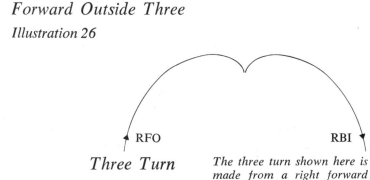

RFO

RBI

Three Turn

Diagram 3

The three turn shown here is made from a right forward outside edge (RFO), but threes can be executed from all edges. The one shown here is the most useful one to learn at this stage.

inside edge, if you can skate backward on one foot properly, you will hit it automatically after the turn.

Let us take the turn on the right foot. Strike onto a forward outside in the first position. After you have traveled a few feet, bring your free arm, shoulder, and hip strongly forward and press your skating arm and shoulder back (Illustration 26A). While you do this, *it is very important to keep your free foot back and as nearly in the original position as possible.* As you are on a curve, you will be making part of a circle, and it is important that, as you turn your shoulders, you look directly toward the center of this circle. There will come a point where, if you have rotated your shoulders and hips strongly enough, you can flick your skating foot around onto a back inside edge. As your foot turns you must immediately press your free arm, shoulder, and hip back as in 26B, which was taken just as the foot had turned. The head is still looking toward the center of the circle. The free arm, shoulder, and hip continue to press back while the head may either stay looking toward the center of this circle or turn to look along the line of travel, as in 26C. For a beginner it would be better to continue to look toward the center of the circle. Hold the back inside edge as long as you are able. Notice how the whole of the free—that is, the left—side is in a very strong open position. Another view of the position just before the turn is shown in 26D. The shoulders have not yet reached their fully rotated position, but the illustration shows how the free foot is kept strongly back despite the rotation of the upper part of the body.

77

At first it is a good idea to try this turn at the boards, as in Illustration 27, A, B, and C. Here the skater is trying the turn on the left foot. Stand close to the boards, about a skate's length away. You will have to do it practically on a straight line, but this does not matter while you are getting the feel of things. Push off parallel to the boards as in 27A, with your left hand holding the barrier. Now bring your right hand around onto the barrier, look at the wall (27B), and make the turn. Illustration 27B shows very clearly how the free hip is pressed forward before the turn. After the turn, you should still be looking at the wall, as in 27C.

Before we go any further, here is some more skating language. A three turn, like other turns you will meet later on, is divided into three parts: the *preparation,* or *prepared position,* immediately before the ◄ turn (26A), the turn itself, and the *check,* or *checked position* (26C). Check is the reversal of the rotation that is deliberately set up to make the turn. Look at Illustration 28F. Here the skater has not checked her shoulders, and you can see that the free arm is now forward instead of back. If you don't check after the three you will simply go on turning and you will spin, come to a stop, or fall over.

Errors. We will deal first with errors into the turn. The most common is failure to turn the shoulders sufficiently before the three. This is shown in 28A, which you should compare with 26A. This makes the turn almost impossible because there is no pressure to turn the foot and, if you do succeed in getting it around by a jumping action, you are in completely the wrong position to make any attempt at the edge after the turn.

A. *Start close to barrier,*
holding with left hand

B. *Place right hand on*
barrier and make the turn

C. *After the turn; note*
that skater still looks
at wall

In 28B the skater has succeeded in making the turn but has pitched up onto the toe pick of her skating foot. Well, you were warned. This results simply from not having learned to skate backward on one foot! There is no shortcut to this.

A horrible fault and its likely result is shown in 28C and 28D. The skater has allowed her free leg to swing forward before the turn. Ten chances to one with someone first learning the three the free leg will continue its swing around and up as in D, leading to a very nasty fall. You must keep your free foot somewhere on a line behind the skating heel before, during, and after the turn.

A good preparation is shown in 28E, but the head is looking in the wrong direction. When the three is done in this way, it is almost impossible for a beginner to maintain the back inside edge after the turn.

If the preparation is correct, there are two main errors that occur after the turn; 28F shows the obvious one of failing to check the shoulders, but 28G shows a very subtle one that is a frequent cause of trouble. Every part of the body has been checked correctly except the hips. Look at 28G closely and you will see that the left hip is being allowed to pass forward instead of being pressed back. The hips are

78

Errors in the Forward Outside Three   *Illustration 28*

A. *Shoulders and hips not*
sufficiently rotated.
Compare 26A.

B. *Lack of skill in back-*
ward skating has caused toe
scratch after turn

C. *Swinging the free foot*
forward before the turn . . .

D. *may result in a very*
nasty fall

closing. Look again at 26C and you will see that the skater is correctly pressing the free hip back after the turn; the hips are open.

The forward outside three is the most commonly used turn in figures, ice dancing, and free style. The methods of executing it differ somewhat according to the purposes for which it is used. In ice dancing, for example, you would be required to keep the feet much closer during the turn and obtain much of the rotation from the hips, while for advanced figure skating a varied number of techniques are employed to get the turn "clean." Don't worry about this at the moment; the movements just described give the general principles.

79

When you can make a reasonable attempt at this turn, you will have learned a lot about the mechanics of skating and will be ready to go on to another very intriguing one, the *mohawk*. This curious name ◄ came from the supposed resemblance of the turn to a movement performed in the war dance of an Indian tribe living in the Mohawk Valley in New York State.

Forward inside open mohawk

This movement is very similar to a three. Again, it is a turn from forward to backward on a curve, but this time you change feet as the turn is made. There are several types of mohawk, but the easiest to learn and the most commonly used is the one starting on the forward inside edge. Although it is more commonly used starting on the right foot, you will be shown it on the left foot so that you can more easily compare the illustrations with those of the forward outside three, which the mohawk so closely resembles.

This turn is usually referred to simply as an inside mohawk, because

E. *Head looking in wrong direction before the turn*

F. *Skater has failed to check rotation of shoulders after turn*

G. *Correct, except: free hip not checked after turn*

the closed version is very rarely used. It is an "open" mohawk because of the position of the free leg after the turn. Incidentally, advanced skaters who may wonder about this should study the hip positions of the open and closed outside mohawks described in Chapter 22.

Start in the first position for a left forward inside edge as in Illustration 29A. After traveling a little distance, bring your free foot into a position at right angles to your skating foot so that the heel of your free foot is opposite the instep of your skating foot. As you do this, rotate your shoulders strongly just as you did in the three. You should now be approximately in the prepared position, as shown in 29B. Now place your free foot on the ice, ball of the foot first, and, as you do so, extend your left foot quickly along your line of travel, at the same time pulling the whole of the free side strongly back. This is the checked position shown in 29C. You should now be on a back inside edge, and the position is exactly the same as if you had just executed a forward outside three. Compare Illustration 29C with 26C (p. 76).

If you want an easy, flowing turn, the key to the whole movement is the strongly prepared position just before the turn. It is this position that is so hard to get at first, but a really full preparation will prevent any tendency of the blade to skid as it is set down on the ice. Unlike the three, it is possible to learn this turn without a strong shoulder rotation, but it is not advisable, and you will find that the method described gives the best results in the long run.

To get the feeling of what you are doing with the feet, try the inside mohawk at the boards in a similar way to the three. Start close to the boards, push off on a very shallow inside edge running almost parallel to the boards, bring your free foot into position, put both hands on the boards, and make the turn.

80

A. Start on left forward inside, first position

B. Prepared position just before turn: note position of left hand

C. Immediately after turn: free side is strongly checked

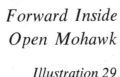

Forward Inside Open Mohawk

Illustration 29

Notice that, just as in a three, the skater looks toward the center of the circle immediately before and after the turn. One of the remarkable things about this turn is that before placing the free foot on the ice you do not have to turn it out any more than is shown in 29B. If you put it down on the forepart of the blade, your forward movement and the action of the free leg taking up its position will turn your blade for you. The old idea was to turn the foot out as much as possible before the turn and put it down heel to heel as in 29F. This is known as a *spread-eagle* mohawk and is to be avoided.

◄ **81**

There is one tip that is extraordinarily helpful. When you get into the prepared position just before the turn, bring your skating hand sufficiently far around so that it is directly above your free foot. This is a difficult position to achieve, but if you can do so and hold the position for at least a second you should get a beautiful mohawk.

Errors. All the faults that are made before and after mohawks are almost identical with those before and after threes; 29D, for example, shows lack of shoulder rotation and the skater is looking in the wrong direction. Other faults that mohawks and threes have in common are throwing the free leg up in front as the turn is made, rising up on the toe after the turn, and failure to check some part of the body. There are, however, a few errors that are peculiar to the mohawk. The spreadeagle mohawk has already been mentioned. Another fault is leaning away from the circle, as in 29E. Also, avoid swinging your free foot forward first and then bringing it back into position to make the turn. This would then be termed a *swing mohawk* and, although not actually a fault, it ◄ is a difficult habit to correct when later on you might want to use the turn in ice dancing and a swing mohawk is not called for.

As you become a stronger skater you will probably find that you

Errors

D. *Wrong: not enough rotation of shoulders and hips before turn*

E. *Wrong: skater is leaning away from turn*

F. *"Spread-eagle" mohawk: old-fashioned, unacceptable in official tests*

can execute this and other turns with less *apparent* preparation. However, in the learning stage all movements should be very definite and deliberate.

Learning a back outside edge

82

To complete this chapter you are going to be given a tip on how to get onto a back outside edge. You just don't hit this edge as naturally as a back inside. Don't worry too much about shoulder positions right now. You will be given the key first positions for both this edge and the back inside in Chapters 11 and 12. This will give you time enough to get the feel of these edges before tackling the first positions, which are quite tricky.

Start moving backward on a circle in a counterclockwise direction, bring both feet together, and try to continue the curve. Look to the center of the circle you are making, press your right arm slightly back and your left arm forward, and try to get all your weight over onto the right foot, as in Illustration 30A. Now gently allow your left foot to take a position behind, as in 30B. Keep the weight on that part of the blade between the middle and ball of the foot. You should now be skating on a right back outside.

The main errors are flinching away from the curve due to timidity (30C) and trying to make the curve with the feet too far apart (30D), which prevents you from leaning at all.

Practice this edge constantly both on the right and left foot so that you will know a back outside edge thoroughly by the time you get to Chapters 11 and 12.

Learning a Back Outside Edge Illustration 30

A. *Skate a backward curve on two feet, weight on right foot*

B. *Carefully allow left foot to take up position behind*

C. *Flinching away from curve; keep skating hip pulled in*

D. *Feet too far apart, making it difficult to lean*

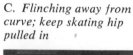
— Errors

9. Consecutive Forward Edges

Consecutive forward outside edges

You are now going to learn to use your forward outside edges to progress across the ice in a series of half circles. This is far less complicated than anything you learned in the last chapter, but it has been necessary to wait until you were sufficiently strong on your outside edges before tackling this movement, which requires a controlled change of shoulder positions.

Diagram 4 shows the pattern of what you are about to do. Notice that these half circles are symmetrically grouped around an imaginary straight line extending across the ice. This is known as the *long axis*.

Assume you are going to skate these half circles across the rink, starting on your right outside edge. See the long axis in your mind's eye extending across the rink and stand at right angles to this line in the starting position for a forward outside edge (Illustration 31A). Make a thrust onto the outside edge, and as soon as you have it under control (which by now should be almost immediately!) slowly start to pass your free leg forward. Just after your free foot has started to move forward, release your shoulder position so that at the quarter circle (31C) your shoulders are in a neutral position and your free foot is just passing the skating foot. The free foot continues on forward as in 31D. At this point do not allow the shoulders to rotate too strongly.

Consecutive Forward
Outside Edges

Illustration 31

A. *Preparing to start from rest at right angles to long axis*

B. *Strike onto a right forward outside edge*

Diagram 4

Start from rest →

RFO

LFO ← *Imaginary line forming the "long axis"*

Direction of travel

Note that each edge is started at right angles to the long axis. The diameter of each curve should be about three times the skater's height.

C. *At the quarter circle, pass the free foot forward*

F. *Strike onto left forward outside, new shoulder position fully assumed*

E. *At long axis bring the feet together and bend both knees*

D. *Approaching long axis, shoulders start to assume new position*

Just before the axis bring your feet together, bend your knees, and start to assume the first position for the next edge, as in 31E. The thrust is made almost straight back, not to the side as in general stroking. This will help you to start the edge in the proper first position. As the new edge is started, the arms and shoulders will have completed their movement, so that you are now on a left forward outside in the first position.

Apply these instructions to the left foot and continue in this way across the rink. If the curves you are making have a diameter of about three times your own height, in a standard size rink of 185 feet by 85 feet, it is possible to get in five half circles across the rink, three on the right foot and two on the left, assuming you started on the right foot. Although in official tests it is usual to skate these edges across the rink, there is no reason why the length of the rink should not be used for practice. It is not advisable, however, to try to skate them around the ends of the rink. The fact that the long axis has now become a curve shortens the length of the edges on the inside of the curve and lengthens them on the outside. This inequality in the length of the edges prevents a strike being made at right angles to the axis, and one of the main points of the exercise is lost.

Errors. The thing to remember in each half circle is not to rotate the shoulders too early and not to take up the new first position fully until the knee bend starts, just prior to the thrust. If your shoulders rotate too early or too strongly, it will be almost impossible to stop them, and you are likely to start the new edge badly out of position, as in Illustration 32A.

All this assumes that you are striking onto each edge in the correct direction, which at first attempt is highly unlikely. To make true half circles, you must strike at right angles to the axis. In Diagram 5 the skater has started correctly but has struck in the wrong direction on the following edges, owing to having failed to turn the thrusting foot out correctly. This fault can also be due to the beginner's ingrained conviction that to make a curve he must twist his body in the direction of the curve instead of just leaning. To correct this, at the moment of thrust look in the direction in which your striking foot is pointing, as the skater is doing in 31A and 31E.

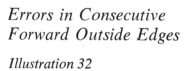

Errors in Consecutive Forward Outside Edges

Illustration 32

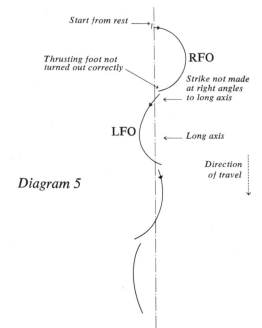

Start from rest

RFO

Thrusting foot not
turned out correctly

Strike not made
at right angles
to long axis

LFO

Long axis

Direction
of travel

Diagram 5

When the strike is made at the wrong angle,
the skater eventually loses his long axis

A. *Shoulders overrotated before thrust, feet not together*

B. *Thrust made with toe pick, shoulders out of position*

C. *Wrong shoulder forward before strike onto new edge*

Another error is not to bring your feet neatly together before the thrust, which usually results in a toe push, as in 32B. It is most important that, after the free foot has been swung forward, it is brought back level with the skating foot. In 32C the skater has failed to rotate the shoulders at all and is starting the new edge in the wrong position. Since the skater is skating in good form, why is it wrong to do the half circles in this way? It is wrong because it encourages all the faults that you have up till now been at pains to avoid. Remember that an experienced skater who has his body well under control can take liberties with his positions and techniques that would be very unwise for a beginner.

The half circles you have just learned have been done in the form of ➤ *swing rolls.* The word "roll" simply means an outside edge on one foot immediately following an outside edge on the other. A swing roll is an edge during which the free foot is swung past the skating foot and then returned alongside it for the next thrust. If you ever take any official figure skating tests, you will be permitted to do these consecutive edges with or without the swing of the free foot. However, the method shown here—with the swing—is the more common.

Consecutive forward inside edges

Illustration 33 should make it clear that pretty nearly everything that has been said regarding the forward outside half circles applies equally to the forward inside. You start, of course, in the appropriate position for a forward inside. Bring your free foot slowly forward after the push, carefully change your shoulder position, bring your feet together, bending your knees and completing the shoulder position as you do so, and then strike onto the new edge.

The errors are basically the same as in the outside edges: overrotation of the shoulders, failure to bring the feet together at the axis, striking in the wrong direction, and, of course, pushing with the toe. As with the outside, the inside edges can be done as plain rolls or as swing rolls, but the swing roll prepares you for movements you will use if you take up ice dancing or skate figures later on.

It should be mentioned that during both the outside and the inside swing rolls you should rise on your skating knee as the free leg swings forward. This allows room for the free leg to pass the skating leg in a good position. Both knees bend again before the new thrust. Also, although the free toe is pointed out and down at the beginning and end of the swing, the blade of the free foot should pass the skating foot parallel to the ice surface. If you continue to point your free toe directly down toward the ice as it passes, you will have to bend your free knee in a very ugly manner to allow the foot room to pass. Here is another tip if you want your skating to look elegant: the free foot, when it is behind, is usually turned out at about right angles to the curve, but when it is forward it is turned out to a much lesser degree. Illustration 21 (pp. 64–65) of the key positions offers good examples.

Those readers interested in ice dancing are now equipped to learn the basic dance movements explained in Chapter 19.

B. *Immediately after thrust: note free foot slightly inside curve*

A. *About to start on right forward inside edge from rest*

Consecutive Forward Inside Edges

Illustration 33

Long axis

C. *Free foot passing forward at the quarter circle*

D. *Approaching long axis, shoulders square to line of travel*

E. *At long axis bring feet together and bend both knees*

F. *Strike made onto new edge*

10. The Waltz Three and Drop Mohawk

Waltz three

This movement consists of a normal forward outside three, after which you change feet, placing the free foot down onto a back outside edge, thus continuing the original curve. Diagram 6 shows the appearance of the tracing on the ice. It is called a *waltz three* because it is used ◄ in one of the oldest ice dances, in which partners do a succession of these threes around each other to waltz tempo. When the change of feet takes place relatively quickly after the three, this movement is sometimes known as a *dropped,* or *drop, three*.

The movement looks comparatively simple, but the tricky part comes when you try to control the back outside edge, particularly immediately after the turn. In Illustration 34 the first three positions, A, B, and C, are simply a repeat of the forward outside three. In D the free foot is being placed on the ice, and in E the right foot has left the ice, leaving the skater on a back outside edge. Stop and examine these two photographs. Notice that the arms, shoulders, and hips are still in the same position as they were in C. This should be shouted to the heavens! The position shown in E is one of the most important in backward skating. It is the key to the control of the back outside edge. After you have held this position for a short distance, the body is allowed to rotate until it reaches the position shown in H. There are several generally accepted ways of doing this, but probably one of the best is that shown here, which is designed to control that old enemy, swing. First allow the free

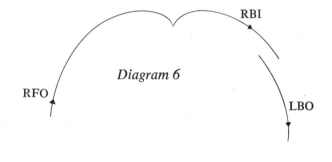

Diagram 6

90

Waltz Three

Illustration 34

A. *Preparing to make the turn from the right forward outside edge*

B. *The turn is made. Note position of free foot during turn.*

C. *Strongly checked position after turn: note position of head*

D. *Left foot placed down onto BO, no change of body position*

E. *Right foot leaves ice, still no change of upper body position*

F. *Free leg passes back; shoulders turn slightly but stay under control*

G. *The head is turned smoothly but right arm is still kept forward*

H. *Right arm and shoulder allowed to pass back; free side now "open"*

leg to pass back as in F, still keeping the head looking into the circle and the free shoulder forward. Now turn the head, followed smoothly by the shoulders, as in G and H. You can, of course, move the whole of the free side around in one piece, but it is not such a good exercise in controlling the edge. However, there are other good methods, and, if you are taking lessons and your instructor has strong ideas on the subject, he probably feels his method suits your skating best.

The distance that an experienced skater holds the back inside edge after the three before putting his free foot down depends on the purpose for which he is using the turn. At first, try to hold the back inside for two or three feet, but a lot depends on your speed and height. It is very important to see that you are in control of your back inside edge before changing feet, otherwise you certainly will not control the following back outside.

91

Errors. The main fault at first is allowing the whole of the free side to swing around as the free foot is placed down, as in Illustration 35A. There are variations of this, as shown in 35B, in which the skater has allowed her head and shoulders to swing around at the same point. Bad form caused by the skater's bending forward at the waist is shown in 35C, and in 35D she is kicking the free foot in the air as she takes up the back outside edge. All these are common errors, but that shown in 35A is the worst.

Errors on the Back Outside Edge of a Waltz Three

Illustration 35

A. *Whole of free side allowed to swing back at beginning of edge*

B. *Free foot correct at beginning of edge but shoulder allowed to swing*

C. *Bad form: "sitting on the edge" instead of standing erect*

D. *Free foot kicking up at start of back outside edge*

Forward inside drop mohawk

This movement bears the same relation to the plain inside mohawk as the waltz three does to the three; the *drop mohawk* is a forward inside mohawk followed by a change of feet onto a back outside edge. (The name drop mohawk is recently coined and may be unfamiliar to some skaters, but it is a short and convenient term.) If you can do a forward inside mohawk and have learned your waltz three properly, there is nothing new to learn. Make your mohawk (Illustration 36, A, B, and C), and when you are on the back inside simply change feet by

92

Forward Inside Drop Mohawk Illustration 36

A. *Start on a left forward inside edge, first position*

B. *Prepare for turn, upper part of body well rotated*

C. *Check free side of body strongly after turn*

D. *Maintaining checked position, place free foot onto a BO edge*

E. *Keep shoulders checked while change of feet is made*

F. *Turn head smoothly while holding shoulders checked (see text)*

G. *Now release shoulders. Whole of free side is now open*

placing your free foot down onto a back outside. Compare 36 D and E with 34 D and E. The skater is putting his foot down in the same way as the skater doing the waltz three. The positions look a little different because of differences in skaters' style, but in essentials they are the same. The skater doing the drop mohawk is turning his head a little sooner, but he is still holding a very strongly checked position. In the next two photographs you will see that his method of changing position is slightly different. He moves his head first and then the whole of the free side, but he has already established control, as shown in 36F, so the movement is a perfectly sound one. For learning purposes, however, we advise that the same timing be used as in the waltz three.

93

In both this movement and the waltz three, be careful how your free foot comes off the ice when taking up the back outside edge. As it is lifted off the ice it should take up a position slightly outside the curve, with the free heel more or less pointing toward the skating toe (36 E and F).

The obvious fault of swinging the shoulders around as the change of feet is made is shown in Illustration 37A, and 37B shows the free leg swinging back at this same point.

You may now go ahead, if you are so minded, and tackle the move- ◄ *ments described in Basic Free Style, Chapters 14, 15, and 16. You have also reached the stage where you should try the forward eights described at the end of this book (Chapter 24).*

Errors on the Back Outside Edge of a Drop Mohawk
Illustration 37

Note similarities to errors in a waltz three

A. *Head and shoulders swing around at start of back outside edge*

B. *Free foot allowed to swing back at start of edge*

11. Back Outside Edges, Crossovers

Back outside edge from rest

When traveling backward, we make the thrust quite differently from the forward thrust. Power is obtained by a semicircular cutting action from the back inside edge of the thrusting foot.

As a preliminary exercise, skate backward in a counterclockwise direction on two feet, keeping them close and level. Bend your knees, turn your heel out, and, without picking it up off the ice, make a semicircular cut with the back inside edge of this foot, returning it immediately to the side of the skating foot. Repeat this a number of times in both directions, clockwise and counterclockwise, until you have a good feeling for the movement. Try not to scrape your toe picks on the ice.

94   Now try the same action from rest. Assume the thrust is to be made from the left foot onto the right back outside edge. Stand with both feet a little over a skate's length apart with your arms turned slightly toward the right, as in Illustration 38A; in 38D the skater is standing with the right foot turned out and just the toe picks touching the ice. This is the more elegant position, but if you ever take any tests you must stand with both blades flat on the ice, as in 38A; the position shown in 38D is now illegal.

Sway your weight over onto the left foot, at the same time lifting your right foot, bringing it up to the left foot as in 38B, and allowing your arms to move slightly to the left. Make a semicircular cut with the back inside edge of your left foot, striking onto a right back outside

C. *Strike onto RBO. Skater is about to make semicircle toward camera.*

B. *Place weight on left foot, pick up right, and bring feet together*

A. *Stand with both blades on the ice, weight on both feet*

D. *A more elegant starting position but now illegal in official tests*

Back Outside Edge from Rest

Illustration 38

E. *Free side swinging around as thrust is made. Compare with C.*

F. *Weight transferred too soon from left foot, which has not completed thrust*

Errors

edge and at the same time rotating your shoulders strongly to the right, as in 38C. Complete the action of the left foot by drawing it in toward the right foot. As soon as your left heel points to your right toe, lift your left foot off the ice.

Note that at the start the skater is facing the camera and that after the thrust she is starting a back outside edge that will describe a semicircle toward the camera. When the left foot has completed the thrust and has left the ice, the skater will be in the first position for a back outside edge. This is the same position as that immediately after the change of feet in the waltz three or drop mohawk. Once again the skater is in that very strongly checked position that is so important in backward skating. Although there is no actual turn on the ice when the thrust from rest is made, we say that the position is checked because the skater is trying to stop a very strong rotation set up by the thrust.

What makes this thrust difficult is the fact that, as the left foot makes the semicircular cut, it is moving in a counterclockwise direction, which tends to pull the body around in that direction, as shown in 38E. This is just what you don't need if you want to keep the edge under control. So, as your left foot makes this movement, you must turn the whole of your upper body plus your hips in a clockwise direction, as in 38C. Although it seems quite unnatural and impossible at first, you must push your left hip strongly forward as you make the thrust. If you do this properly, your left foot will leave the ice in a forward position; it should never leave the ice level with or behind the skating foot, as it is about to do in 38E.

Mention should be made of the way in which your weight passes from your thrusting foot (in this case the left) to your skating foot. Keep your weight over the left foot as long as you can and transfer the weight gradually. This timing is a very difficult thing to describe in words. Your movement from rest actually starts when your right foot is still in the air; your left foot should travel a few inches before the right foot touches the ice. As the right foot is set down on the ice, the weight of the body is still not over it because the thrust is just starting. During the semicircular movement of the left foot, the weight is evenly

96

transferred to the right foot. If you throw your weight too soon over onto the right foot, you take all the power away from the left foot, which no longer has any proper contact with the ice. It is a general principle in skating that to get full power from a thrust, whether you are skating forward or backward, the weight stays over the thrusting foot until the last possible moment (see pp. 45–46).

The effect of getting the weight too soon onto the skating foot is very nicely demonstrated in 38F. The left foot has come off the ice almost immediately after the thrust was started. The left heel is actually still turned out but, if the blade is not in contact with the ice, it obviously cannot be making a thrust. The fault as shown is, of course, exaggerated and usually occurs in a far more subtle form.

97

A good tip is to turn the thrusting heel out in a pigeon-toed fashion just as the feet come together immediately before the thrust.

Now reverse all the foregoing instructions and work on the start from rest onto a back outside left.

Consecutive back outside edges

The same general principles of pattern hold good as for the forward half circles, but, as you have just learned, this time you start facing down the long axis. Diagram 7 shows the appearance of the tracings on the ice.

Start from rest as you have been shown, being careful to strike onto your back outside at right angles to the long axis. Hold your first position under control for a moment, then slowly pass your free leg back, allowing the whole of the body to rotate with it until you reach the position shown in Illustration 39D. Note that this time you are being allowed to turn the whole of your body in one piece. In these half circles this makes for a prettier action, and, if you have practiced your checked positions, you should by now be able to take a few liberties with your back outside edge and still remain under control. Here again, however, if you overrotate your shoulders you will be in trouble.

Bring your feet neatly together, bend your knees, press your left

B. *Strike made onto RBO. Left foot has not quite completed thrust.*

A. *Skater square to long axis about to skate curve toward camera*

Diagram 7

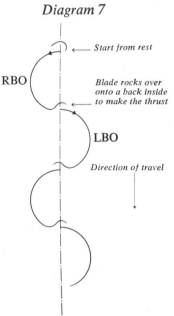

Start from rest

RBO

Blade rocks over onto a back inside to make the thrust

LBO

Direction of travel

Consecutive Back Outside Edges

Illustration 39

Long axis

C. *Body rotates gently; free leg passes back at quarter circle*

D. *Approaching long axis; note open position of free side*

E. *Compare body position during moving thrust with that in A*

F. *Strike made without pause onto new edge*

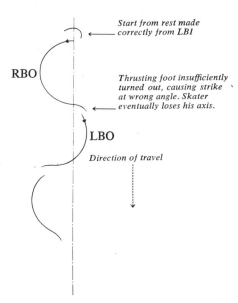

RBO

Start from rest made correctly from LBI

Thrusting foot insufficiently turned out, causing strike at wrong angle. Skater eventually loses his axis.

LBO

Direction of travel

99

shoulder back, and make the new thrust at the axis (39E). You will see that the lower part of your body is in a different position from the initial start. This makes it a little more difficult to turn the thrusting foot out, but the principle of the action is the same.

There are two very common faults which usually occur at this point, both resulting in the new strike's not being made at right angles to the axis. The first is failure to turn the heel of the thrusting foot out fully; the second is that of rotating the whole body in the same direction as the thrusting foot, causing the strike on the new edge to be made at the wrong angle to the axis (Diagram 8). The best cure for these faults is to be made aware of the fact that you are committing them. If you can find some clean ice, compare the tracings you are making with those in Diagram 7, and then do your best to make the necessary corrections.

To help control your positions on the back outside half circles, remember that at the beginning of each edge you will be looking down the axis, your general direction of travel. This also prevents bumping into people. For official test purposes, these consecutive back outside edges may also be done with or without the swing of the free leg. This does not, of course, apply to dance tests that may specifically call for a swing roll.

Back crossovers

This movement consists of moving backward in a circle by means of crossing one foot across and in front of the other. Although the back crossovers are usually taught earlier in a skater's career, you will make a much better shot at them now that you have learned a proper back thrust.

Start moving backward on both feet in a counterclockwise direction with your right shoulder in a strongly checked position and your head looking toward the center of the circle you are making, as in Illustration 40A. Make a semicircular thrust with your left foot (40B), but this time instead of lifting it off the ice continue the movement by drawing it across and in front of the right foot, as in 40C. The right foot is now lifted off the ice (40D) without a toe scratch and placed not against the skating foot, as in the forward crossovers, but inside the curve and behind the level of the left heel, as in 40E. The movement is then repeated indefinitely. The strongly checked position is maintained throughout, which, apart from anything else, allows the skater to see where he is going. Illustration 40F shows the cross viewed from the direction of travel.

This method gives maximum power and speed over the ice, and it is interesting to note that, as one moves counterclockwise, the left foot never loses contact with the ice and vice versa. This is the way the more powerful and experienced skaters execute the movement, and, if you have learned your back edges properly, you too can use this method. When it is learned at an earlier stage, the beginner is more likely to pick the left foot up and over the right, which gives a clumsier look to the movement. As with the forward crossovers, you will eventually learn to get an additional thrust from the outside edge of the foot that has crossed behind, but this is an advanced movement obtained through a subtle weight transference that only comes after very considerable practice. If you try to do it now, you will probably just succeed in scraping your back toe picks over the ice.

Back crossovers must also be practiced in a clockwise direction, which

C. *leaving left foot in contact with ice, draw it across right*

B. *Make semicircular thrust from left back inside edge and . . .*

A. *Skate backward in a counterclockwise curve*

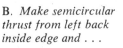

Back Crossovers

Illustration 40

D. *Keeping right side strongly checked, pick right foot softly off ice . . .*

E. *and place on ice well to inside of curve. Repeat the movement.*

F. *Crossover at C shown from different angle*

you might find a little easier. In this case it will be your right foot that is brought in front of and across your left. Start by moving backward on both feet in a clockwise direction with your left shoulder and arm pulled strongly back in a checked position along the line of travel. Keeping your head looking to the center of the circle you are making, thrust with the back inside edge of your right foot and, still keeping it in contact with the ice, draw it across and in front of the left foot. The left foot, which will now be on a back outside edge, is lifted quietly off the ice and placed onto the ice well inside the curve and behind the level of the right heel. The left foot is now once more on the back outside edge. Repeat the movement by thrusting from the right back inside.

102

➤ *You may now complete the remainder of all chapters in the sections on Basic Free Style and Basic Dance Movements.*

12. Back Inside Edges and a Change of Edge

Back inside start from rest

The illustrations of the back inside start from rest have been combined with those of the half circle that follows it.

This start, shown in Illustration 41, A, B, and C, differs from that of the back outside only in that you stand with your back to the long axis and lean in the opposite direction. Stand on the flat of your blades with your feet apart and arms slightly to the right, as in 41A. Rock over onto the left foot, lifting your right foot off the ice and bringing it up to your left, at the same time allowing your arms to move slightly to the left (41B). Make a semicircular thrust with your left foot, turning your arms to the right and keeping your left shoulder forward, but now you must lean into the circle so that you strike onto a back inside edge (41C). Draw your left foot in toward the skating foot, and the initial movement is completed (41D).

Due to the action of the thrusting foot, the natural swing at the start of this edge tends to be in the opposite direction to that of the three other edges. The usual error, therefore, is that shown in 41I, where the skater has allowed her left shoulder to pull strongly back at the moment of thrust. Compare this with the position shown in 41C.

A. *Start back to long axis, about to make curve toward camera*

B. *Weight on left foot, pick right foot up and bring feet together*

C. *Make semicircular thrust with left foot, striking onto RBI*

D. *Immediately after start, note left heel pointing to right toe*

Consecutive Back Inside Edges

Illustration 41

Long axis

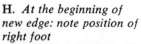

E. *At the quarter circle draw left foot level with right, and . . .*

F. *turn left heel out ready to strike onto new LBI edge*

G. *Strike onto new edge. Note similarity to "sculling" action (p. 49)*

H. *At the beginning of new edge: note position of right foot*

I. *Free shoulder pulled back at end of thrust; compare with C*

Error at start of back inside edge

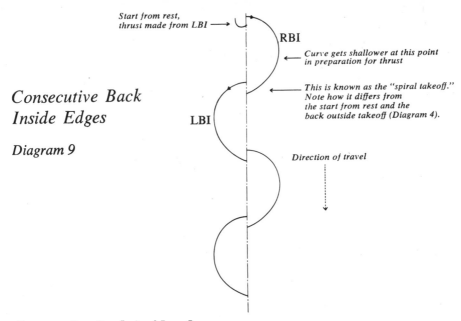

*Consecutive Back
Inside Edges*

Diagram 9

Start from rest,
thrust made from LBI →

RBI

← Curve gets shallower at this point
in preparation for thrust

← This is known as the "spiral takeoff."
Note how it differs from
the start from rest and the
back outside takeoff (Diagram 4).

LBI

Direction of travel

Consecutive back inside edges

Once you have made the start from rest onto the back inside, all similarity to the back outside half circles ceases. It is *not* usual to do this movement as a swing roll, and in the consecutive half circles the thrust, once in motion, is quite different from that of the back outside.

After the thrust from rest, the position is held for a moment (41C) until control is gained, and then the free foot, having left the ice, is brought slowly into a position alongside the skating foot while the head and shoulders move slowly to the left (41E). Just after the feet have been brought together (usually just after the quarter circle has been reached) the free heel turns out, is placed on the ice at right angles to the axis, and the feet make a sculling action (Diagram 9). If you turn back to Illustration 12 (p. 49), you will see the similarity to one of the methods mentioned for moving backward across the rink. During this sculling action the weight is gradually transferred to the left foot, and the right arm and shoulder press forward (41F and 41G). The right foot is drawn in to a forward position and lifted off the ice. You should now be on a back inside, as in 41H. Continue the half circles by the same movement and sculling action.

This method of thrusting from one back inside to another while in movement is known as the *spiral takeoff*. In tests this is the official ◄ method when skating back inside half circles. However, if you take up figure skating later on, you will use a method similar to the start from rest, even when in movement.

Fundamentals

Change of edge

This is a rocking movement from one edge to another and forms a serpentine pattern on the ice. It can be done from any edge; if you start on an outside, you finish on an inside, and vice versa. These changes are used in all types of skating. The one you will be shown here is made from the right forward outside to right forward inside. (The abbreviation would be *RFOI*.)

➤

Start as for a right forward outside swing roll (Illustration 42, A and B), but this time as the free foot is passed forward the left shoulder presses back, as in 42C. You should not reach this position until just before the axis, and then, as the axis is reached, you swing your free foot back and press your free shoulder forward. As you do this, rock over onto an inside edge and you will find yourself in the first position for that edge. An alternative position to 42D in completing the change is shown in 42E. In this case the shoulders do not change position. Both methods have their merits.

This change is not difficult to make, and the usual errors are not serious unless you use the movement in a figure, when what now appear minor errors will assume major proportions.

Diagram 10 shows what good and bad changes look like if you look at their tracings on clean ice. You will make nice changes if you do them as described and do not kick your free foot up before the change; the free foot passes forward as in a swing roll, but you should not lift it any farther before the change. Also, do not deepen the edge before the change. By this, we mean, do not suddenly allow your edge to get on a sharper curve just before you change edges. This is the fundamental error that causes most bad changes. Also bear in mind that the change will take place instantaneously, the moment you think about it and change your position; you don't have to go into a lot of contortions several feet before the change to make it come about. Another thing to ponder is the fact that the change of position of the free foot does not make the change of edge; it simply puts you in a position that is comfortably and easy to hold following the change. But we are going too deeply into the subject. Just do as you have been told and you will make a nice change.

106

A. *Start on a right forward outside edge as for a half circle*

Long axis

B. *Pass free foot forward at the quarter circle, but . . .*

Change of Edge

Illustration 42

C. *as you approach axis keep free shoulder pressed back*

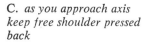

D. *Swing free foot back, reverse shoulders, and rock onto an RFI*

Diagram 10

E. *Alternative position after change: shoulders do not reverse*

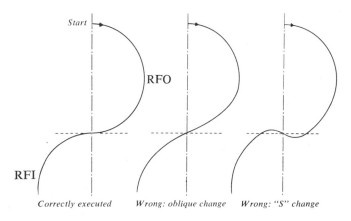

Start

RFO

RFI

Correctly executed   *Wrong: oblique change*   *Wrong: "S" change*

Part III

13. A Spin, a Jump, and a Spiral

Choosing your direction

Up till now you have been told to practice all movements on both the right and the left foot or, with movements involving both feet, clockwise and counterclockwise. You will now find that most skaters, even advanced ones, spin and jump in one direction only. Even those skaters who can spin and jump both ways tend to have a strong preference for one particular direction and concentrate on it. This does not matter, as at the moment it is not required either in tests or in competitions that you spin and jump both ways, although some skaters do so occasionally in an attempt to score a few more points. Just how successful this is remains at present a moot point. You are advised to choose one direction and stick to it until you have mastered the jumps and spins covered in this book. If eventually you go on to competitive skating, you will probably be taking lessons, in which case you should take advice on whether any particular jumps and spins should be learned in the other direction as well.

The choice of direction is an important one, and you may need some help in deciding which is the better for you personally. If you have no one to help you decide (a competent instructor can usually spot which is your natural direction), try the spin described here, and particularly the waltz jump in Chapter 14, and try to decide which is the better for you. It is very important at this early stage that you spin and jump in the same direction. Don't spin clockwise and jump counterclockwise, or vice versa.

By far the majority of skaters spin and jump in a counterclockwise direction, but there are many who do the reverse, including a number of champions. There is one great advantage, however, in jumping to the left, or counterclockwise: the normal flow of the traffic in all rinks is counterclockwise and, as jumps are approached with a fast-moving start and usually on a curve, you will be moving with the general flow of skaters if you jump in this direction. If you jump to the right, or clockwise, you will be moving against the general flow and may have to wait a long time before you find sufficient space to jump. I remember a pupil who was practicing before a competition with thirty-four others and she was the only one who jumped clockwise. I don't think she managed to practice a single advanced jump satisfactorily during the whole period.

In all the jumps and spins illustrated in this section we have kept to a counterclockwise direction, but if you find your natural direction is the other way you had better hold this book up to a mirror.

Two-foot spin

The two-foot spin is the simplest spin of all and is done on two feet on the flat of the blades, which means it is not done on the toe pick, as are many spins you will learn later.

First Method. Stand with both feet apart, left toe on the ice, and turn your head and shoulders very strongly to the right, as in Illustration 43A. Throw your arms and shoulders to the left, bring your right foot around and close to your left, which will drop onto the flat of the blade, bring your arms in, and try to spin, as in 43B. (It would be better if you had your feet a little further apart than is shown here.) The thing that prevents most people spinning when using this method is that they do not continue to bring their right arm round as they throw themselves into the spin. The right arm stops somewhere out to the side and the spin is cut short. During the spin your weight should be toward the ball of the left foot and the heel of the right.

Second Method. This is the better but far more difficult method. If you can do it, you will learn a lot about spinning and it will prepare you for the action of a spin on one foot later on.

Start by skating forward on two feet on a fairly small curve, with your left foot forward and your feet well apart (44A). You will be on an outside left and inside right. Now throw most of your weight over onto the left foot, bending your left knee strongly as you do so and trying to make a smaller and smaller circle. While you do this, it is important to keep your right foot back and quite a long way out of the circle you are making on your left foot. (Illustration 44, A and B, shows the position). As the circle gets smaller, your left hip will push out to the

110

A. *With left toe pick on ice, turn arms and shoulders well to right*

B. *Throw arms and body around to left and try to spin on flat of blades*

Two-foot Spin: First Method

Illustration 43

Two-foot Spin: Second Method   *Illustration 44*

A. *Skate forward curve counterclockwise on two feet*

B. *Throw weight over left foot; keep right foot back and to side*

C. *Force curve into small circle, keeping right foot wide*

D. *At smallest point of curve, swing right foot round and spin*

side so that, although you are leaning on a strong edge, the top part of your body is nearly vertical to the ice (44C). As your circle gets smaller and smaller there comes a point where you must spin. Just as you feel this point and not before, let your right foot swing around in a wide circle and into position alongside your left foot; straighten up on both knees and pull your left hip in so that you are standing straight. If you are now spinning, you can pull your arms in for increased speed.

The main fault is trying to spin before you have forced your left blade round into a tiny circle. Another common error is to bring your right foot directly up to your left without letting it make a large circle. You must think of your right foot as swinging out and around in front of you as it is brought in. Don't go into this spin too fast; the speed of the spin depends on the wide separation of the feet as you enter it and, of course, the right timing.

111

Bunny hop

The bunny hop is one of the few jumps in skating that does not require a turn in the air. Take a little speed and skate forward on the flat of your left blade in a straight line. Throw your right leg well forward and land on the right toe. As you land, push with your right toe and continue on the left foot, again on the flat of the blade so that you finish in the same position as you started (Illustration 45, A through D).

Simple as it is, young skaters have a hard time getting the idea of it. Instead of coming down on the right toe, they land on the flat of the right blade, which is not the safest thing to do. It often helps children if they think of jumping across a little stream. In this way they get the idea very quickly.

Bunny Hop   Illustration 45

A. *Skate forward on flat of blade, skating knee well bent*

B. *Throw free leg forward and jump from left knee*

C. *Land on right toe pick (not on flat of blade!) and . . .*

D. *push with toe pick onto flat of left blade*

A. *Note how hands and arms are held level with shoulders*

B. *Side view—back well arched, free foot level with head*

C. *Wrong: no comment should be necessary*

The usual fault in this jump is to throw the free leg forward with the free knee strongly bent instead of keeping it straight, as in 45B. Bending the free knee in the air makes the jump look absurd and gives the skater the look of a prancing horse.

112

Forward spiral

➤ Now is the chance for all who have "done ballet" to shine. A *spiral* in skating is similar to an arabesque in ballet. The word "spiral" originally referred to the pattern that was usually made on the ice when skaters assumed an arabesque position. They would start on a very large circle that covered practically the whole rink and then hold this position while the circle got smaller and smaller, thus forming a spiral pattern on the ice. Skaters today have so many jumps and spins to get into their competition programs that they cannot afford to spend all this time in one position; spirals, therefore, got shorter and shorter until the word came to mean the position itself.

Try it at first in a straight line with a strongly arched back. Ideally your free foot should be as high as your head, as in Illustration 46B. The free knee should be as straight as possible with your free foot turned out. When you think your free knee is straight, really straighten it—it will always go a little farther; 46A and B show the skater in a very good position. Notice how erect the head and shoulders are. In 46C, the skater is showing the typical first attempt of an average beginner. When you are trying the forward spiral, be sure to keep your skating heel pressed firmly into the ice; otherwise, in attempting to get a good position, you are likely to come onto your skating toe and fall flat on your face! This spiral should be practiced on both the right and the left foot.

14. Fast Drop Mohawk and Waltz Jump

Drop mohawk at speed

This movement, which you met in Chapter 10, is done in two distinct ways. In ice dancing very neat and close footwork is required, while in free style there is a wider separation of the feet in order to get a flowing and powerful action. Done in this way, the drop mohawk is frequently used as an approach to certain jumps. It is this latter method of executing the movement that concerns us here.

Get up some speed by means of several forward crossovers in a counterclockwise direction and strike onto a fast right forward inside edge. Now stretch your free foot well inside the curve you are making, so that your free heel is opposite the instep of your skating foot with a distance of at least the length of a blade separating the feet. Make the mohawk by putting your foot onto the ice just where it is: don't pull it back to the skating foot before the turn. After the mohawk, you will be on a left back inside. Keeping a strongly checked shoulder position, step well inside the curve with your right foot, placing it on the ice behind the level of the left heel. As you do so, make a thrust from the left back inside edge. Illustration 55E (p. 133) shows very well the action of stepping into the circle with the right foot and making the thrust with the left.

Basic Free Style

The movement may now be completed by rotating the body outward into an open position, finishing with the head looking in the direction of travel. It is important that this last position be held under control and that an uncontrollable swing not be allowed to develop. If you have trouble preventing swing on this back outside edge, take your free foot back first, keeping your free arm and shoulder forward; then turn your head, and finally allow your free shoulder and arm to pass back. The free arm should be kept fairly low and close to the body.

You can give an attractive style to this whole movement by making a slight change of edge, or sway, from the left forward outside edge to a left inside just before stepping into the mohawk. This swaying movement is performed in the following manner: After your last forward crossover you will have made a thrust onto a left forward outside edge; at this point swing your right foot slightly forward and sway over

Waltz Jump   *Illustration 47*

A. *Start on an LFO, left shoulder slightly forward, arms low*

B. *Swing free leg up and push with left, make a half turn in air*

C. *Land on an RBO, left arm forward, head facing where you came from*

D. *Arms in "neutral," also good if firmly held (see text)*

E. *Landing in an "open" position, effective but tricky*

Two alternative landing positions

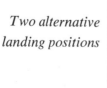

onto the left inside, bringing your left arm and shoulder forward as you do so. Bring your feet together again and make the thrust onto the right forward inside.

It is a good exercise to practice the fast drop mohawk in the other direction as well. But if you have decided to do your jumps counterclockwise, you will have more use for the drop mohawk in that direction.

Waltz jump

The *waltz jump* consists of a jump from a forward outside edge directly to a back outside on the other foot, thus making a half turn in the air. Although this jump is so-called because it bears some resemblance to a waltz three done in the air, the turn is started by the free leg and not by the shoulders. In fact, you should do exactly what you were told not to do in the waltz three: start the turn by throwing your free leg forward. (Illustrations 47, A and B

Assuming that you have decided to do your jumps and spins in a counterclockwise direction, the best way to approach the waltz jump at first is to take a right forward outside edge and then step onto a left outside, swing your free leg forward with the free toe turned slightly in, and make a very small hop onto the right back outside.

When you have plucked up enough courage to do the jump more as shown in Illustration 47, there are some very important points to think about. As you approach the jump on the left outside, drop both arms a little but keep your left shoulder forward (47A). The free leg is now thrown forward and up, pulling the whole of the free side after it; at the same time a lift of the arms assists in getting height.

Errors

F. *Pushing free arm forward and looking into circle before jump*

G. *Turning head outward on landing, causing lack of control*

H. *Dropping free side on landing: you may skid off your edge*

Errors. The common error of turning the shoulders first is shown in 47F. Another very common fault is straightening far too soon the knee from which the jump is being made. You should jump from your skating leg as the free leg starts the upswing; in this way one leg assists the other. Another fault is that of trying too hard to turn; if the shoulders are allowed to follow the free leg, its action of swinging forward will automatically start you turning.

116

As you land on your back outside, look firmly in the direction from which you came, with your free arm and shoulder held forward in a firmly checked position, as in 47C; do not land with your head already turned as in 47G. It is also very important to land with your hips square to the line of travel. Never allow your free hip to pull back on the landing. Please remember this, as it is a fault that is difficult to see and is often overlooked.

Another very common fault is shown in 47H, where the skater has allowed the whole of the free side to drop. This throws the weight of the free leg inside the curve you are making and will probably cause your blade to skid and result in a fall. Keep your free side lifted on the landing; do not allow it to collapse.

There are many jumps in skating, the vast majority of them landing on the back outside edge in a similar way to a waltz jump. It is worthwhile, therefore, to study this landing in some detail.

There are two other arm and shoulder positions on the landing that some instructors favor. One is a neutral position, as in 47D, and the other a very open position, as in 47E. Personally, I like a beginner to use the fairly checked position in 47C, where he can actually see what he is doing with his free arm. Provided that it is strongly held, the neutral position in 47D is also very good. The open position in 47E is a pretty and effective one, but if a skater does not learn to check the shoulders when he is first learning to jump, he may run into serious trouble later on in advance jumps that require more than one turn in the air. It is important to note that the one thing all three positions have in common is the position of the head, which should look firmly along the curve in the direction from which the skater came. If the head is turned on the landing as in 47G, your back outside edge will probably cut in on a small circle and the position will be impossible to hold.

It is vitally important that a jumper appear well in control of his landing edge or the effect of the jump is lost, however high or fast it is done. After you land, stay absolutely still and let the edge run for sufficient distance to demonstrate that you are actually in control of the landing. If your free leg is in a good stretched position on the landing, don't drop it weakly toward the ice; keep it absolutely still. If the jump is not as good as you might have hoped, don't look apologetic and flop; stay still and pretend it was a good one; probably only you could tell that it might have been better. If you fall, learn to roll over and get up again in one action; don't sit on the ice trying to clown it off. The best of skaters fall, and if you see a professional show skater fall you are lucky, because he gets up so quickly that if your attention had been distracted for a fraction of a second you might not even have known it had happened.

When you think you know what you are doing in the waltz jump, you can try approaching the jump with the drop mohawk done as explained in the beginning of this chapter. After getting up a little speed, do your drop mohawk, which will bring you onto a back outside. Then simply step forward onto a forward outside edge and jump. The important thing here is that on the back edge just before you step forward there must be no swing. The back edge must be absolutely under control. If your shoulders are swinging while you are on the back outside, they will continue to swing as you step into the jump, and you will get the fault shown in 47F.

117

15. Toe Loop Jump, Inside Pivot, and Outside Spiral

Toe loop jump

The majority of skating jumps go directly from one edge to another but some are assisted by the toe pick, as is the one you are about to learn. The alternative names for this jump are *cherry flip* and occasionally *tap loop jump*. It is shown in Illustration 48.

From a back outside edge (48A) stretch your free leg back, start to turn your shoulders and strike the toe of your free foot into the ice (48B), continuing the turn and jumping into the air to land on the back outside (48D). Everything you have been told about landing in the waltz jump applies here. The action of tapping your left toe into the ice should be a smooth one, with little or no pause on the tapping toe. To get the idea of it, you can think of making a waltz jump off the toe.

118   *Toe Loop Jump*   *Illustration 48*

A. *After an FI three you are on an RBO; stretch free foot back*

B. *Tap left toe pick into ice and jump to left*

C. *Make one turn in the air and . . .*

D. *land on original RBO edge with shoulders in checked position*

Notice in 48A the direction in which the skater is looking just before the tap. This is a good but quite difficult way to learn it. At first it helps if you turn your head more over the left shoulder before the tap.

The errors here are mainly those that apply to jumping in general, but one word of caution is in order. When making the tap, you must see that your toe points firmly down toward the ice; otherwise, your pick may fail to dig in, which usually results in an unexpected fall.

The commonest way to get onto the back outside before making this jump is by turning an inside three. They are not difficult, so you might as well try one. The same principles apply as for a forward outside three: there is the prepared position, the turn, and the check. If you are a counterclockwise jumper, take a right forward inside in the first position, rotate your arms and shoulders strongly counterclockwise, and make the turn, checking your shoulders strongly as you do so. As the turn is made, allow your free leg to pass around in a fairly wide arc, so that you finish in the position shown in 48A. If the toe loop jump is done from an inside three, there is very little, if any, pause before the tap, and the whole movement is a continuous flowing one.

119

Forward inside pivot

Pivots can be made into attractive little movements, and there is a ◄ pivot corresponding to each edge. The simplest of all is the forward inside. Take a forward inside edge on quite a small curve, stretching your free foot well inside the circle. Your free arm will be back and your skating arm forward. The position is almost identical to that just before the fast mohawk in the last chapter, the difference being that you should be traveling much more slowly and on a small circle. Assuming you are on a right inside edge skating counterclockwise, allow your left toe pick to touch the ice very lightly and, when you have traveled a few feet, put more weight on the toe, bend your left knee, and, allowing your right skate to continue on a large curve, pivot around your toe.

The thing to note in this, as in all pivots, is that you must not try to pivot too early. For several feet the pivoting toe will lightly touch the ice, moving over the surface as it does so. If your inside edge travels on a smaller and smaller circle, there will come a point where it is quite easy to throw your weight over the pivoting toe. If you try to pivot before this point is reached, the movement is almost impossible. Done properly, this pivot can be used as an entry into a two-foot spin.

Forward outside spiral

If you have mastered a good spiral position as shown in Chapter 13, you should now try it on an outside edge, as in Illustration 49. This should be practiced on both the right and left foot.

There is no particular difficulty here that you did not meet when trying it on a straight line, except that natural swing may cause your free leg to pass outside the curve. Keep the free leg well pressed back over the tracing.

As you become a better skater, you will eventually learn spirals on all edges and with a variety of arm positions. At this point you can also try the forward inside. In this spiral it is a good idea to have your free arm forward with the skating arm out to the side. This helps to keep the edge under control and makes it look a little different from the outside spiral.

Beginners have an automatic tendency to drop the arms, so you should think of keeping them fairly high. When going into a spiral it is a good idea to lift the free leg first as far as it will go before allowing the top part of the body to drop into position. Keep the top part of the body erect and lift your free leg so that a definite angle is created at the waist. As you take your position, this angle at the waist must not change or else you will get a bad position, with your seat making a hump as you lower the upper part of your body. Do try to keep your chin up and your eyes looking straight ahead.

120

Forward Outside Spiral

Illustration 49

Same position as in 45A but you are now on an LFO edge

16. Mazurka and Salchow

Mazurka

The mazurka is another jump assisted by the toe pick, but this time involving only a half turn in the air. Illustration 50 shows the movements.

Start on a back outside right and tap your free toe into the ice as you did in the toe loop jump (50A). This time, however, notice the open shoulder position before the tap and the fact that the head is looking outside the circle. As you jump into the air, cross your right foot in front of the left (50B) and land on the right toe, pushing as you do so onto a left outside (50C and D). Notice that the head moves very little during the jump and that the landing is in a strong left forward outside first position.

If you jump the other way around (that is, clockwise), you will, of course, have to reverse all these directions. However, for the purpose of description, it is better to assume one particular direction of rotation. This allows the use of the terms "right" and "left foot" instead of "free" and "skating foot." The latter terms can be confusing when both feet are on the ice at the same time.

There are numerous variations to this jump: you could, for example, land just as easily on your toe and push onto a left inside instead of outside, in which case the jump would have a serpentine pattern. Or

A. *Start on an RBO, stretch free foot and arm well back*

B. *Tap left toe into ice and jump; cross right foot in front of left*

C. *Land on right toe pick; lower part of body has made a half turn*

D. *Continue the movement by a thrust onto an LFO edge*

122

E. *Alternative position at top of jump, right foot behind* left

Mazurka   Illustration 50

you can take off from a right back inside and finish on a left forward outside. These variations are fun to work out and do. The position in 50E shows an alternative position at the top of the jump. Here the right foot is crossed behind the left instead of in front. This variation, if performed strongly, is sometimes called a *scissors* or *scissor jump,* especially when executed with a pronounced cross.

The mazurka is a very simple jump and should be practiced in both directions.

Salchow

The salchow is a much more advanced jump. In the United States it is pronounced "sal-cow" and is named for the former world champion Ulrich Salchow, who is credited with its invention.

From a back inside left the skater swings the free leg in a counterclockwise direction across the tracing, rotates in the air, and lands on

A. *Start with an LFO three, free foot stretched well back*

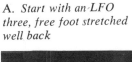

LBI, *usually with slight swaying action*

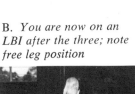

Three turn

Direction of rotation ⤴ ← *Edge deepens*   LFO

Diagram 11

Landing edge, RBO

B. *You are now on an LBI after the three; note free leg position*

C. *Throw free leg in front of body and across curve, turning to left*

Salchow

Illustration 51

D. *Continue movement by jumping into the air and . . .*

E. *land on an RBO in a strongly checked position*

F. *On LBI after three: same position as B, but shown from front*

the right back outside edge as in a waltz jump. The correct tracing is shown in Diagram 11.

The method of getting onto the back inside is usually to turn a forward outside three. Illustration 51A shows the skater entering a left forward outside three with the free foot kept very far back along the tracing. As the three is made, the free leg maintains this wide position. When approaching a salchow never make the three with the feet close, as this ruins all rhythm through the jump. However, immediately after the three the swing of the free leg must be stopped, or at least slowed down, so that the position on the back inside edge (as shown in 51B and 51F) is held for some distance before the free leg is thrown around for the jump.

Errors. Beginners invariably swing wildly when turning the three, allowing this swing to continue unchecked and take them around the jump. In most cases the swing is so violent that the back inside edge is reduced to a distance of two or three inches instead of at least three or four feet (Diagram 12). Remember that the three is not part of the jump; it just serves to get you onto the back inside edge. The rotation for the jump is obtained from deepening the back inside as the free leg

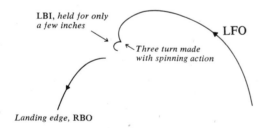

LBI, *held for only a few inches*

LFO

Three turn made with spinning action

Diagram 12

Landing edge, RBO

Errors in Salchow

Illustration 52

A. *Free leg too high after three; head should not check (compare 51F)*

B. *Free leg too close to skating leg: it should pass in a wide arc*

is swung around (see Diagram 11). This takes quite a bit of practice, and at first you will come up on the toe instead of making a deeper edge. You can increase your control of the jump by turning the three and seeing how far you can hold the back inside before jumping.

The other main errors are shown in Illustration 52. In 52A the skater has swung her free foot too high after the three. (Compare this position with the correct one shown in 51F.) She will not be able to hold this position because she has already lost control of the back inside. This illustration also shows the less common fault of checking too much after the three, and the head is turned in the wrong direction. When a three is used as an entry to the salchow, it is important to note that the point at which the free side is checked is much later than after a regular three, and that the head looks directly up the line of travel rather than to the center of the curve. Comparison of the positions shown in 51B and 51F with that in 34C (p. 90) should make this clear.

In 52B the skater has not carried the free foot around wide enough at the jump, making a very cramped affair of it. This is often caused by having the feet too close together at the three.

It is very common for a skater to use a drop mohawk before the three leading into this jump. Having arrived on a back outside edge after the drop mohawk, simply step onto a forward outside and make the three. But do keep each edge under control, particularly the back outside after the mohawk; otherwise a strong swing can develop during the three, robbing you of all mastery of the back inside edge before you jump.

Don't forget that, as with all back outside landings, it helps to land with your hips square to your line of travel. Beware of allowing your free hip to pull back on the landing.

125

17. One-foot Spin, Back Outside Pivot, and Step

➤ *Do not attempt any movements in this or the following chapter until you have mastered Chapters 3 through 11 in the section on Fundamentals.*

One-foot toe spin

Although you had to start by learning a two-foot spin, you will now find that nearly all skating spins are done on one foot, some on the flat of the blade, others on the toe. The one described here is the commonest of all and is known simply as a *toe* or *scratch spin*.

Again, it will be described as though you are rotating counterclockwise. Just to get the feel of it, start with a two-foot spin; when you are steady, lift the right foot and rise up on the toe of your left, which should leave you spinning on that foot. When you can do this, you will learn to enter the spin on a strongly curved left forward outside edge. Here is a description of the entry and the spin as it should be done; various points and difficulties will then be discussed.

Start by making a waltz three on the right foot, allowing the free foot to pass fairly wide at the turn. Keep the head looking strongly into

C. Force edge into very sharp curve until spinning point is reached

B. Step onto strong LFO, arm and shoulders turning into "neutral"

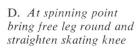

A. Back crossover onto RBI, left arm forward, head looking to left

One-foot Toe Spin

Illustration 53

D. At spinning point bring free leg round and straighten skating knee

E. Start spin by bringing free foot in front of left leg (see text)

Diagram 13

LFO

A. Correctly executed spin. Centering is achieved by the sharply spiraling curve of the entry edge.

LFO

B. Wrong: failure to force entry edge into spiraling curve has caused the spin to "travel"

Error

F. Free foot pressed down for speed; this needs considerable practice

G. Exit from spin on RBO. Note similarity to landing from jump (47D)

H. Skater has failed to pull in skating hip at moment of spin

the circle and make a deep back crossover, allowing the left arm and shoulder to rotate to the right, as in Illustration 53A. Now step onto a strong left forward outside (53B), bringing your arms and shoulders square to your line of travel and looking with the head to the left. Your left knee should be strongly bent and the left hip pressed into the circle you are making. The right foot is allowed to leave the ice (becoming the free foot) and swung in a wide arc, while the curve made by the left outside is forced smaller and smaller (53C and Diagram 13A). If you can force this edge around into a small enough circle, there comes a point where you must spin. As this point is reached, bring the free leg smartly forward, straighten your skating knee, pull your skating hip in, and rise up on your toe until the lowest pick is just scratching the ice. Try to hold this position for one or two turns and then bring your free foot into a position either behind or in front of the skating knee, as in 53E. The spin is usually learned at first by bringing the free foot in to the back or side of the skating knee. For really fast spins, however, the free foot is brought in front and then lowered to the position shown in 53F. At the same time, the arms are pulled in. Both of these actions increase the speed of the spin, but the lowering of the foot in front requires considerable practice and balance.

The great difficulty in all spins is centering them, which means keeping the spin going on one spot and not "traveling" over the ice. One of the most common causes of traveling is trying to spin too soon, by which is meant trying to spin before your skating edge has been forced into a small enough circle. Diagram 13B may help to make this clear.

A common error is shown in 53H, where the skater has failed to pull her left hip in and therefore cannot stand straight in the spin. The whole of the right side is dropped, and ten chances to one she will not be able to center the spin or get any great speed. The illustration shows the fault grossly exaggerated, but even a hint of it will cause considerable trouble. The more advanced skater should also think of tilting the hips —that is, the whole of the pelvis—forward; any slight backward tilt will take away from the speed of the spin.

You should learn to come out of this spin in exactly the same position as you would out of a jump. Just before you want to finish the spin, open the arms, check the shoulders, change feet, and allow your free foot to pass back in a wide arc into its final position (53G).

Avoid spinning too high on the toe. Only the lowest toe pick is used, and the scratching action should be quite a light one. If you look at the marks on the ice you will see that the toe pick makes very small circles, and it is interesting to note that during this spin the blade is actually traveling backward.

At first, one of the great worries of the beginner is dizziness. With time and practice you will find this becomes less and less of a problem, as your body learns to adjust. To reduce dizziness it helps considerably if, as you come out of the spin, you fix some object in the rink with your eyes. Never spin with your eyes closed. Lastly, for the benefit of those who have studied ballet, it should also be mentioned that it is not usual or advisable to "spot" when spinning on ice.

129

Back outside pivot

This is quite a difficult movement but very effective when done at speed. However, it must be learned slowly and carefully.

Get onto a back outside edge by means of a waltz three or a forward inside three, keeping your free arm well forward. Now reach back inside the circle with your free toe and, after allowing it to scratch across the ice for a short distance, pivot around it; illustration 54A shows the position. It is essential to get the free knee well back into the circle. The common error is shown in 54B, where it can be plainly seen that

A. *Start on sharp RBO; reach well back into circle with left foot*

B. *Wrong: free knee outside curve, making pivot impossible*

Back Outside Pivot

Illustration 54

the free knee is outside the circle. When the back outside pivot is done in this way, the feet can get tangled up in a very unpleasant manner.

In all pivots the toe pick is usually carried lightly across the surface before being firmly inserted into the ice. On the back outside pivot the ankle should be turned over slightly to allow this. Although this turning of the ankle is difficult to see in the photograph, a few experiments will give the feel of the movement.

In former years this pivot was commonly used as an exit to spins, but this is now considered rather old-fashioned. Nowadays it is usually done fast, in a broad sweeping movement over a large section of ice. When the back outside pivot is executed at speed, the free leg is held back very strongly inside the circle, the toe pick scratching lightly over the ice surface for a very considerable distance until the circle is small enough for the actual pivot to be made.

130

A standard step sequence

When you can jump and spin strongly enough and have mastered some spirals and a few other movements, you may want to put them all together into a connected program skated to music. But before ➤ you do so, there is another part of free style known as *footwork* to be considered. This consists of sequences of turns and edges that are used to

A Standard Step Sequence
Diagram 14

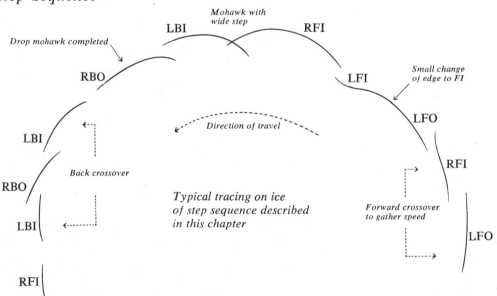

link together highlights of the program and assist in gathering speed over the ice without too much obvious effort. Nowadays many of these steps (sometimes called *dance steps*) are so complex and require such a high degree of skill that they rate as high or higher than some of the more difficult jumps and spins. There are many standard sequences which, when learned, will give you a basis on which to make up your own.

One of the simplest is done as follows: After skating several forward crossovers in a counterclockwise direction, go straight into a forward inside drop mohawk, as was described in Chapter 14. When you arrive on your right back outside edge, keep your checked position and stay looking into the circle you are making; do not continue the movement outward. While holding this strongly checked position with the shoulders, pass your free foot behind the skating foot onto a left back inside. As it goes behind, it should not pass across the line of travel; just pass it to the rear. Step into the circle with your free foot, placing it onto a right back outside, and pass your left foot across your right onto a left back inside. This movement is simply a back crossover. Still keeping the same shoulder position and with your head still looking into the circle, step from the left back inside onto a right forward inside to finish the sequence. Diagram 14 shows the sequence of edges and the pattern made on the ice.

If later on you take up ice dancing with a partner, you will learn that this step sequence, done much more precisely and with closer footwork, makes up the final series of steps that the man does in a dance called the "Fourteenstep." However, the vast majority of step sequences used in free style are not to be found in ice dancing, although some of them are suitable if adapted to the broader type of footwork that is usual in free style. The sequence just described is very useful for gathering speed and taking you around the end of the rink in a flowing movement.

131

18. Loop Jump, Back Inside Pivot, and Step

Loop jump

In a loop jump you take off from a back outside edge, make one turn in the air, and land on the same back outside edge from which you started; Illustration 55, A, B, C, and D, shows the various stages and Diagram 15 the tracing on the ice. This is not so easy as the salchow as there is very little assistance from the free leg, rotation being obtained almost entirely from a "deepening" (sharp increase of curvature) of the edge just before the takeoff.

The usual approach to this jump is to gather a little speed forward and then do a drop mohawk onto a back outside edge. Most beginners, however, find the jump easier to learn from a waltz three. In either case you will arrive on your back outside in the checked position shown in 55A, with a very strongly bent skating knee. Start to rotate the whole of your body and head evenly by deepening your right back outside edge (55B). As is shown in the illustration, you must keep your free leg forward the whole time. The rotation is continued and the jump is made, still keeping the free leg in front of the skating leg, as in 55C. The landing is made in the usual position, with the free leg passing back to the rear of the skating leg and finishing slightly outside the curve.

A. *Start on an RBO after a waltz three or drop mohawk*

B. *Force edge onto sharper curve and jump to left*

C. *Skater in air halfway through jump*

D. *Land on an RBO in a strongly checked position*

E. *Another view of A; note wide step, whole of body facing inward*

Loop Jump   *Illustration 55*

133

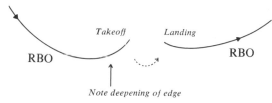

Diagram 15   *Typical appearance of loop jump tracing on ice*

Takeoff   Landing

RBO   RBO

Note deepening of edge

Errors. Illustration 55, B and C, shows very clearly how the body is rotated evenly; avoid twisting the shoulders around before the hips. This fault is shown in Illustration 56A, with the added error that the skater is leaning back along the line of travel. The smooth turning action of the body is only possible when the skater has learned to deepen the edge—that is, to curl the edge in strongly before the takeoff.

A. *Left shoulder pulled back before jump, edge not curved enough*

B. *Right foot placed on ice level with left instead of as in A*

C. *A moment later: whole of free side pulls back, a very bad fault*

Errors in Loop Jump

Illustration 56

A very common and extremely bad fault is that of pulling the free leg (and with it the rest of the free side) back before the takeoff, as shown in Illustration 56C. The fault usually starts immediately after the three or mohawk, with the free foot being placed onto the ice level with the skating foot (56B) instead of back and inside the curve (55A). This is a very bad error indeed and needs a lot of thinking about. There is no doubt that it is possible to do the jump in this way, but the habit, once developed, is almost impossible to break, and if you continue with

134 ➤ your skating it makes the double loop jump almost impossible. A *double jump* is a single one with one more turn in the air added; if you learn the single ones properly you will have far less trouble with the doubles.

Back inside pivot

Get onto a left back inside by means of a left forward outside three, stretch your free leg inside the circle with the free knee straight, and allow the right toe to scratch the ice very lightly. When you feel you are ready, throw your weight over the right toe, bend your right knee strongly, and make the pivot. Illustration 57A shows the moment just after the free knee has started to bend; you can see by the head that the weight is not yet over the pivoting toe. In 57B and 57C the weight is now well over the toe and the pivot is being made in a very effective manner.

Back Inside Pivot Illustration 57

A. *Skate a deeply curved LBI and place right toe pick into ice*

B. *Throw weight over right toe and make pivot on strongly bent knee*

C. *Pivot from different angle: a very effective position*

A second step sequence

This step sequence is a good one, and a lot of speed can be gained from it. Step sequences are difficult to name, but this may be called the "back outside three, mohawk" step. First, however, you must learn a back outside three.

Get onto a right back outside edge and rotate the head and shoulders, keeping the free foot in front as in Illustration 58A. This is the prepared position. Now, if you are rotated sufficiently, flick your skating foot around onto a forward inside, bringing your free arm and shoulder forward as you do so into a checked position (58B). Note that in threes, unlike the takeoff to some jumps, the skater does not deliberately deepen the skating edge.

135

E. *You are now on an RBO ready to repeat the step with an RBO three*

A Second Step Sequence   Illustration 58

D. *place free foot onto an RBO, completing the drop mohawk*

A. *Skate an RBO and turn an RBO three (see text)*

B. *After the three you will be on an RFI; check shoulders strongly*

C. *After the three skate an RFI open mohawk and . . .*

When you can do this back outside three reasonably well, go on to the next part. You are in the position shown in 58B, on a forward inside. Allow your shoulders to rotate, bring your free foot into a position inside the circle opposite your skating foot, and do a mohawk. In this step you will find that it is not necessary to prepare strongly in order to make the mohawk; this is owing to the action of the free leg, which, after the three, is being brought *back* into position rather than forward. You are now on the back inside, as in 58D, from which position you step into the circle with your free foot, placing it down onto a back outside (making a drop mohawk) and turning your shoulders as you do so (58E); this is the same position as the one in which you started (58A). Now you simply turn another back outside three and repeat the step as many times as you wish. Diagram 16 shows the edge sequence and pattern.

At first an uncontrolled swing develops, but this can eventually be controlled by a strong check of the shoulders after the three (58B) and after the mohawk (58D). In order to gain speed there should be a definite thrust from the back inside after the mohawk. It is just the same thrust that is used in the back outside half circles. The step should be practiced in both directions.

A Second Step Sequence   Diagram 16

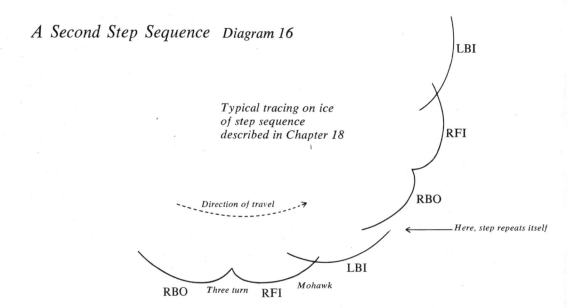

Typical tracing on ice
of step sequence
described in Chapter 18

LBI

RFI

RBO

Direction of travel

Here, step repeats itself

LBI

RBO   Three turn   RFI   Mohawk

Part IV

Basic Dance Movements

19. Forward Outside Swing Rolls, Chassé, and Progressive

The sight of two ice dancers, gliding effortlessly and in perfect unison over the ice surface in rhythm and in time to music, represents for the 'average adult beginner the culmination of all ice skating and the height of his own personal ambition. "If only I were good enough to do just one of the simplest dances, I should be satisfied!" he says. Of course, having achieved his goal he always wants to go on to greater things, but that is beside the point. Quite apart from the attainment of a specific skill, the skating of a dance consisting of rhythmic curves is delightful in itself, especially when executed in harmony with a partner.

In ice dancing are preserved those ballroom dances that were once popular but now are rarely seen: the waltz, the tango, the fox-trot, and the Latin-American group consisting of sambas and rhumbas. Although at present out of favor in the ballroom, these dances still have a life of their own on the ice surface. Of course, the steps must of necessity differ from the ballroom versions, but their original character lives on.

If ice dancing is popular in the United States, it is even more so in Great Britain, where what is known as International Ballroom Dancing (consisting of the above-mentioned dances and others) still has a great vogue. This greatly contributes to the popularity in that country of ice dancing, which parallels that of the ballroom to a great degree. Adding to ice dancing's popularity is the extensive television coverage given to ice events, and in particular to the beautiful formation ice dancing, in which dance couples compete as teams against each other, skating routines that allow separation of partners, novel combinations, and freedom in the holds adopted. Dancing on ice is gaining an ever-growing following in this country and the eventual emergence of a world-champion couple will still further popularize this beautiful branch of skating.

Ice dancing has great appeal to the adult recreational skater, who can get enormous satisfaction from its execution without needing the athletic prowess required to jump and spin or the clean ice necessary for the proper practice of figures. However, lest a wrong impression be created, and in fairness to young American ice dancers who so ably represent this country in international competition, it must be pointed out that ice dancing in its advanced form requires just as much skill and long hours of practice as any other branch of figure skating.

Dances on ice consist of sequences of steps and edges laid out in definite patterns over the ice surface. Most sequences take the skaters halfway around the rink, but a few need a whole circuit for their completion, after which the sequence is repeated indefinitely until the music ends. The design that a sequence of steps makes on the ice is known as the *pattern,* which can be either *set* or *optional.* A set-pattern dance is one requiring that the edges and steps be executed at specific places on the ice surface, while an optional pattern may be laid out in a variety of ways according to the whim of the skaters (in competitions this is not always so, but right now the point is academic).

If you look at the patterns of the three simplest dances on pages 158 to 163, you will notice that they are skated on curves, which, generally speaking, in ice dancing are known as *lobes.* Each lobe may consist of a plain edge or a sequence of edges or steps, all executed on the same curve, which must be completed in a certain number of beats (sometimes called counts) of the music. In ice dancing the most commonly used rhythms are three and four beats to the measure.

The reader who has mastered the movements under the headings of Fundamentals and Basic Dance Movements has the skills necessary to execute the three dances described at the end of this book. He will be able to go on to at least half a dozen more by strengthening his basic skills to the point where he can cope with the increased difficulty of skating the steps with a partner in a dance hold.

Provided you have mastered Chapters 7, 8, and 9 in Fundamentals, ◄
you can learn the movements in this chapter, but wait until you have completed Chapters 10 and 11 before attempting the remaining basic dance movements in Part IV.

Forward outside swing rolls to counts

Looking at the pattern of the Dutch Waltz (p. 159), you will notice that, when used for ice dancing, the swing roll does not occupy a complete half circle. This is because of the increased speed over the ice and the fact that it must be executed in a specific number of beats, which may not give time for the completion of a half circle unless the skater is extremely powerful on his edges. Skating with a partner in a dance hold also produces complications, particularly if you are side by side as in the Dutch Waltz, when you will find that you cannot give such free play to your shoulders as you did when skating alone. When skating with a partner, your shoulders will be held much more square to the line of travel. When skating alone you should practice in a similar way. At the beginning of a forward outside swing roll, therefore, your skating arm should be only slightly in front of your body, and the shoulders will rotate to a far lesser degree than in the full half circles you learned earlier.

When skating the swing rolls to counts, you must still imagine them grouped around an axis, but it is not necessary to start each edge at a complete right angle to this axis. However, each edge will be started at the same angle to the axis as the preceding one. Strong edge skaters will start at a greater angle to the axis than weak edge skaters.

In the Dutch Waltz each swing roll requires two measures for its completion, so it is usually skated to a count of six rather than three.

Strike onto a forward outside on the count of one, keeping your skating knee strongly bent and stretching your free leg behind so that the knee is almost straight. Hold this position without moving until just after the beginning of the count of three, when the free leg should be swung easily forward so that it reaches its position in front of the skating leg at the beginning of the count of four, with the free toe pointed strongly down and turned slightly out. During the forward swing of the free leg, the skating knee straightens smoothly until it reaches a position in which it is very slightly flexed. Just after the beginning of the count of six the free foot is returned to the side of the skating foot, at the same time both knees start to bend, and you are ready to strike off on the first beat of the new measure.

140

This may seem a rather mechanical way of doing it and you may vary this slightly to produce an interpretation of your own, but if you follow the above instructions, the effect should be a reasonably good one, provided, of course, that the action is smooth and not jerky and that you keep your hips forward and your head and shoulders firmly erect. The free leg should remain almost straight during the whole of the forward swing.

Don't stick your toe in the air at the end of the swing or move it as though you were kicking a football. Don't allow your hips to go back —that is, don't stick your seat out—at any time. Keep your chin up and your back straight. This leg and body position is well shown in Illustration 61C. Take a look at the errors in position demonstrated in 61D and shudder! Note particularly how the hips have been allowed to go back. *Keep your hips forward and your head and shoulders erect!*

Your dancing will look much more effective if you can hold the position after a stroke absolutely still, even if only for a very short time. To help achieve this effect, never allow the free foot to drop slightly at the end of the stroke.

Now try the swing rolls to counts of four. The only difference this time is that the free leg starts to move forward just after the beginning of the count of two, reaches its forward position on three, and starts to move back to the skating foot just after the beginning of the count of four, so that the feet are together and the skater is ready to strike onto the new edge on the count of one.

Forward chassé sequence

This is a step in which the free foot is placed on the ice beside the skating foot and the skating foot is lifted slightly off the ice. Following this, a new thrust is made. Although the actual *chassé* technically con- ◄ sists of only two edges, it is usually thought of together with the follow- ing edge. These three edges constitute a *chassé sequence*. It almost **141** invariably, although not necessarily, consists of an outside, an inside, and an outside edge, all skated on the same curve. The movement is shown in Illustration 59. Here the skater is shown starting on a left forward outside (A); the right foot is brought up to the left and placed onto the ice (B); simultaneously the left foot is raised so that the skater is now on a right inside (C); the left foot is placed onto the ice and the new strike made onto the left forward outside (D).

When practiced to the count of four, the first left outside is held for one count; the right inside as the chassé is made, one count; and the last forward outside, two counts. Thus the three edges have been skated during a total of four counts.

When practiced to the count of six, the first left outside is held for two counts; the right inside as the chassé is made, one count; and the last forward outside, three counts. The three edges have now been skated to a total of six counts.

Forward Chassé Sequence *Illustration 59*

D. Place left foot on ice and strike again onto an LFO, forming sequence   *C. Lift left foot slightly, straight up; this is the actual chassé*   *B. Place right foot onto an RFI beside left and . . .*   *A. Start on an LFO with shoulders square to direction of travel*

Forward progressive sequence

The only basic difference between a progressive and a chassé is in the second step. In a *progressive* the free foot is put down on the ice ahead of the skating foot and not beside it. Illustration 60, A through D, shows the basic difference. Originally the forward progressive was a mild form of crossover in which the back foot did the crossing (technically called *tucking*), but in the United States it was later modified for dancing purposes to a movement in which the foot was simply passed, or "progressed," without a crossing action. There is still some difference of opinion as to just how this movement should be executed, particularly between American and British dancers, the latter still tending to make much more of a cross or "tuck" with the back foot. This movement is also known as a *run*, but the term is used mainly by British skaters.

When skating the three edges of a progressive sequence to counts of six, the usual timing is as follows: Hold the first forward outside for two counts, the second step onto the forward inside for one count, and the last forward outside for three counts. When skating to counts of four, the first two edges are held for one count each and the third and final edge for two counts.

Progressive and chassé sequences can be practiced in successive lobes grouped around a long axis or, if space is lacking, in a circle, in which case several would be skated in succession starting on the same foot and then the direction of the circle would be changed to practice them starting on the other foot.

To give character to the progressive and prevent its looking as though it consists merely of plain forward skating, there are two points to be studied. When skating this movement as it is usually made in the United States, don't push with your back foot as you pass your foot forward on the second step. If you do, you will probably push with the toe pick and leave your back foot so far behind that you may be late on the beat for the following edge.

The knee bend is extremely important. To make it as clear as possible,

142

D. *and a strike made onto an LFO to complete the sequence*

C. *The left foot is now picked up and placed beside the right . . .*

B. *but now the right foot "progresses" ahead of the left onto an RFI*

A. *Start on an LFO exactly as for a chassé . . .*

Error

Forward Progressive Sequence
Illustration 60

E. *Rising on second step of progressive, giving "limping" effect*

assume you are starting on the left outside, moving counterclockwise. Start the edge with your skating knee very strongly bent and your free leg straight. As your free leg passes forward, you rise slightly on your skating leg. Your free knee will have to bend very slightly during its forward movement. Now comes the vital part. As your free foot, in this case the right, is placed onto the ice, the right knee should bend strongly but softly as it takes up the weight of your body. It is at this point that the gross error is made of rising on the right knee instead of sinking onto it. This error is shown in Illustration 60E, where the skater is making the additional error of pushing with the toe. The effect is a limping action and is very unattractive. If you have made the movement correctly and are now on a strongly bent right knee, stay down, bring your left foot to the side of your right, and make the thrust onto the final left forward outside. To get the movement you should say to yourself, "down" for the first edge, "slightly up" as the free leg passes forward, "down" as you put your weight onto the second edge, and "stay down" as you make the last thrust.

It is that second edge that does the trick and, if done properly, gives the progressive a beautiful lilting movement. The sinking onto the knee must be soft and controlled, just as though you were lowering yourself onto a spring.

144

For more advanced skaters who may be reading this book, it should be mentioned that there is an increasing tendency to cross these progressives, but the cross is made by the back foot passing across the tracing behind (tucking), rather than by crossing the forward foot in front. When the cross is done in this way, it is possible to get a very good position of the free foot as it leaves the ice. However, if you ever take any dance tests, you should consult your local professional, as it is a controversial point.

➤ *You are now equipped to learn the Dutch Waltz described on pages 158–159.*

D. *Free toe lifted in kicking action, hips not kept forward*

Error

20. Slide Chassé, Back Outside Swing Rolls, Cross Roll

Before attempting this or the remaining chapters on Basic Dance Movements you should have completed Chapters 3 through 11 in the section on Fundamentals.

Slide chassé

Start as for a forward chassé (61A), but this time, as you bring your free foot up to and onto the ice beside your skating foot (61B), pass your new free foot forward as in 61C, which means, of course, that you are now skating on a forward inside. This chassé consists of two simple

Slide Chassé   Illustration 61   **145**

| C. *extend left leg (in the Canasta Tango hold this edge two counts)* | B. *Bring right foot up to left, place it down onto an RFI, and . . .* | A. *Start on an LFO (in the Canasta Tango hold this edge two counts)* |

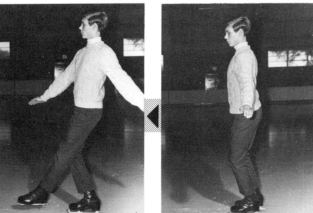

edges, whereas other chassés are usually thought of as a sequence consisting of the chassé itself and the edge immediately following.

You do not often meet this step, but it is a prominent feature of the Canasta Tango (see pp. 160–161), in which both edges of the slide chassé are held for two full counts. The errors are mainly those of position and usually consist of kicking the free foot and toe into the air, at the same time allowing the hips to go back as in 61D.

146   Back outside swing rolls to counts

In this movement, the timing of the free leg swing and the rise and fall of the skating knee are exactly the same as for the forward outside swing rolls except that they are done in reverse. When skating them to the count of six, keep the free leg forward until just after the beginning of the count of three and then swing it easily back so that it reaches its position behind at the beginning of the count of four. During this time the skating knee will straighten to a slightly flexed position, and then both knees bend again as the feet come together.

When practicing to the count of four, start to move the free leg back just after the beginning of the count of two, so that it reaches its position behind on the count of three and starts to move back to the skating foot just after the beginning of the count of four.

Be careful that at the end of the backswing the free foot is not kicked up high. The free toe should finish not more than about a couple of inches above the ice.

Forward cross roll

As was explained in Chapter 9, a simple roll is a curve, usually on a forward or back outside edge, which immediately follows a curve done on the same edge on the other foot.

A forward outside cross roll starts like a swing roll, but at the end of the swing forward the free foot is crossed in front onto the forward outside while the back foot makes a thrust from the forward outside,

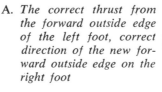

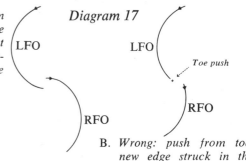

A. The correct thrust from the forward outside edge of the left foot, correct direction of the new forward outside edge on the right foot

Diagram 17

LFO   LFO

Toe push

RFO

RFO

Forward Cross Roll
Illustration 62

B. Wrong: push from toe, new edge struck in the wrong direction

A. *Skater on LFO about to swing free foot past skating foot*

Errors

B. *Thrust correctly made from outside edge of left foot*

C. *Wrong: stepping over instead of around skating foot*

D. *Wrong: thrusting from toe pick instead of blade.*

much as in a forward crossover. The movement is shown in 62A and 62B.

As in crossovers, the free foot should come around the skating foot and not be stepped over it, as in 62C. Also, the thrust must be made from the outside edge with a sideways movement, as in 62B, not with the toe (62D). While the free foot passes around the skating foot, the free toe should be turned in to create a pigeon-toed effect. This helps you start the new edge in the correct direction. Diagram 17A shows the correct and 17B the incorrect tracing on the ice.

➤ The old name for this movement is *Dutch roll,* because this typical rolling action was the method of forward thrust used by the Dutch when skating to market along the canals.

Note that the type of thrust from the outside edge as used in cross rolls and properly executed crossovers is known in ice dancing as a
➤ *cross stroke.*

➤ *You may now learn the Canasta Tango, page 160.*

21. Back Chassé and Progressive, Close Drop Mohawk

Back chassé sequence

The back chassé sequence as shown in Illustration 63 is done on exactly the same principle as the forward one, and the counts are the same. When partners are facing each other in waltz hold (see p. 156) and the girl is doing a back chassé, the man is doing a forward one, so obviously the movements must match in all respects.

When skated to the count of four, the first back outside is held for one count, the second back inside for one count, and the last back outside for two counts. Skated to counts of six, the edges are held for two counts, one count, and three counts respectively. When practicing alone keep a fairly strong checked position with the shoulders as in Illustration 63.

148   *Back Chassé Sequence*   *Illustration 63*

C. Right foot placed down onto an RBO, completing the chassé sequence

B. Bring your feet together, lift right foot (this is the chassé)

A. Start on a right back outside edge

Errors are those of timing and position. Note that when the free foot is forward as in 63A and 63C, the body leans back slightly. This keeps an attractive line through the body and free leg. Although this slight lean back is very effective when the free foot is forward, you must never lean forward when the free leg is back; in this case, keep an upright posture with your hips well forward.

Back progressive sequence

Here again, the back progressive sequence is skated exactly on the same principle as the forward one. If you are skating with a partner and he or she is doing a forward progressive sequence in front of you, the timing, knee bends, and free foot and free leg actions must match exactly. The movement is shown in Illustration 64.

149

As with the forward progressive, there is some considerable difference of opinion as to how the second edge is put down on the ice. It is not so much a question now of to cross or not to cross, but whether the free foot should touch the ice beside the skating foot and slide back along the ice surface into position, or whether it should not touch the ice at all until it is actually behind the skating foot. At the moment of writing, the official *USFSA Rulebook* requires the sliding action, but it is difficult to see how, if done like this, it can match the action of the forward progressive, where there is no doubt that the free foot takes the ice ahead of the skating foot. If you intend to go in for any dance tests, be guided by your local professional.

Back Progressive Sequence   *Illustration 64*

D. *strike onto a right back outside to complete sequence*

C. *Bring feet together and . . .*

B. *Left foot "progresses" past right and is placed down onto an RBI*

A. *Start on a right back outside edge, as for a chassé*

The knee action is the same as in the forward progressive—down, slight rise, down, and stay down—but this is a little more difficult to do backward than forward.

To do the action well the pelvis should be tilted forward; otherwise it is almost impossible to get the proper extension of the free leg on the first and third edges. If you look at Illustration 64, you will see that the extension of the free leg on these two edges (A and D) is greater than on the second edge (B). This also helps to give the movement character and prevents it from looking like a vague shuffle.

150

Forward inside drop mohawk with close footwork

It has been mentioned several times earlier that this mohawk is done with wider footwork in freestyle than in ice dancing. Illustration 65 shows how very close it is necessary to keep the feet when doing this movement in a dance. In order to show this, it has been necessary to take the photographs with the skater coming into the camera instead of across it. In 65A the free heel is practically touching the instep of the skating foot. In 65B the mohawk has just been made and the free foot allowed to extend along the line of travel. The amount of this extension depends on the timing of the dance. In the Swing Dance, for example, where the back inside is held for two counts, the free leg is extended fully, while in a dance requiring only one count to each edge the free foot is not extended so far along the tracing. The next close step is where the free foot is returned alongside the skating foot, as in 65C. This is quite difficult, but a strongly checked position is of considerable help. In 65D, the new back outside edge has been taken up and the free foot extended along the tracing.

Please remember not to swing your free foot forward past the skating foot before the mohawk. Although a swing is not illegal before the mohawk in the Swing Dance, it looks neater without it, and the swing is definitely illegal in most of the other dances.

➤　*You may now, if you wish, go on to the Swing Dance, described on pages 161–163.*

A. *Start a normal FI mohawk by bringing left heel close to right instep*

Forward Inside Drop Mohawk with Close Footwork
Illustration 65

B. *Mohawk is made and free foot extended along line of travel*

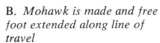

C. *Free foot turned in and placed onto RBO very close to tracing foot*

D. *Movement completed, free foot extended, shoulders checked throughout*

22. Open and Closed Mohawks; Dance Positions

Forward outside open mohawk

You won't meet this mohawk in any of the three dances given in this book, but if you continue on to the more advanced dances you will frequently have to use it. As it is a very tricky one to do well, you might just as well start it now.

As with the forward inside mohawk, it is a turn from forward to backward, but in this case you start on a forward outside edge and change feet to finish on a back outside. The peculiarity of this turn is that while in the forward inside mohawk the feet move in the same direction as a three, in the forward outside mohawk they turn in the opposite direction, against the natural rotation of the curve.

In Illustrations 66, A, B, and C show the movement toward the camera, while D, E, and F show it across the camera.

Start on a forward outside left in a strong first position (A and D); bring your free foot opposite your skating foot so that your feet are at right angles to each other, with the free heel almost touching the skating instep (B and E); at the same time press the right shoulder and hip strongly back. Now place the right foot down onto a back outside, reversing your hips and shoulders strongly as you do so and turning

Forward Outside
Open Mohawk

Illustration 66

A. *Start on an LFO (the skater is traveling toward the camera)*

B. *Bring right heel to left instep, press right shoulder back*

C. *Press left shoulder back, place right foot onto RBO and look to left*

Same positions as above, seen from outside curve

D.

E.

F.

your head to look along your line of travel (C and F). Of all these movements it is the action of the hips that is the most important. Say to yourself as you go into the turn, "right side back," and as you put your foot down, "left side back."

In the final position on the right back outside, the free leg is back and therefore in an open position. Because of this final position it is called an *open mohawk*. There is a prevalent idea that open and closed ◄ mohawks are so termed because of the final position of the hip, but the

A. *Start as for an open mohawk on a left forward outside*

B. *Bring right instep to left heel and rotate both feet so that . . .*

C. *right foot passes behind left onto an RBO. Free hip is kept back and open!*

Forward Outside
Closed Mohawk

Illustration 67

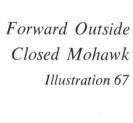

next section will show that it is the position of the free leg that determines whether the mohawk is open or closed.

Forward outside closed mohawk

As regards the actual edges skated, this is the same mohawk as the open mohawk, but because the free leg is passed to a forward position after the turn and is therefore "closed" it is called a *closed mohawk*.

154

Start in exactly the same way as for the open mohawk but instead of bringing the free foot to a position opposite the skating foot, bring the *instep of the free foot* up against the *heel of the skating foot,* as in 67B. If you press the whole of the free side back strongly enough, you can rotate the heel of the right foot slightly so that it will easily slip onto a back outside and, because of the position of the feet, you can simultaneously pass your left leg in front of your right into the position shown in 67C. However, to control the edge after the turn you must press your free hip (in this case, the left) back strongly, just as you did in the preceding mohawk. Your hip, therefore, is now open, although your free leg is closed. This theory may come as a shock to many readers, but there is no doubt at all that it is so. If you press your hip forward with the free leg after the turn—that is, close the hip—it will be almost impossible to hold the edge afterward. (To my more advanced readers, I should like to point out that the closing of the hip

Dance Positions   Illustration 68

A. *This hold is used in the Dutch Waltz and is known as "Kilian" position*

B. *Man's hand firmly on hip of partner, girl presses her hand firmly on man's*

C. *Kilian position reversed, used in Canasta Tango*

coming out of a closed mohawk is the very error that makes the lady's mohawk in the Fox-trot and Silver Tango so difficult.)

More advanced ice dancers should also note that this pressing back of the free hip is not necessary in the Rocker Fox-trot mohawk, because the rotation continues, clockwise, and does not need to be checked.

The closed mohawk may also be executed with a swing forward of the free foot before the turn and is then known as a "forward outside swing closed mohawk." In this form it is met in the Silver Tango, where it is done from a right forward outside by the lady. As in the Fox-trot mohawk, the free hip must be pressed back or opened on the left back outside after the turn. Without this opening of the hip the skater starts a slow rotation in the wrong direction and cannot step forward to the following right forward inside three.

155

Dance positions

Illustration 68 shows those positions, also known as *holds*, that you ◄ will need to know when learning the three dances in the following section.

Kilian position is shown in 68A. The man's hand is firmly on the hip of his partner, and it is important that she assist the hold by pressing her hand strongly on the man's, as in 68B. This is the hold used in the Dutch Waltz.

A similar hold is shown in 68C, but the girl is now on the opposite

D. *Closed, or waltz, position, used in Swing Dance*

E. *Closed position from side. Note erect carriage.*

F. *Closed position showing position of hands and arms*

side. This is known as *Kilian position reversed* (or reverse Kilian position) and is used in the Canasta Tango.

Closed position (also known as *waltz position*) is shown in 68 D, E, and F. This hold is used in many dances, not necessarily waltzes; it is the hold used down the sides of the rink in the swing dance. Note the position of the man's hand just under the girl's right shoulder blade, and also the position of the girl's left hand on the front part of the man's right shoulder. The arms and shoulders should form one firm unit so that the man is able to lead and, when necessary, communicate his speed to the girl, particularly when she is skating backward and is unable to thrust strongly.

156

Illustration 69 shows errors in the Kilian and waltz positions. The common faults are weak posture, slouched shoulders, hips back, no firmness in the arms or body. In the Kilian hold the right hands are not on the girl's hip, and the left arms are slackly held in an indefinite position. The same would, of course, apply to the Kilian position reversed. In the waltz position the girl's left hand is over the back of the man's shoulder so that any forward movement on the part of the man cannot be communicated to the girl. The man's right hand is far too low.

Before starting the sequence of steps that make up a dance it is usual to take several introductory steps to get up speed, during which both skaters come into the hold appropriate to the dance; Illustration 68 G shows the *hand-in-hand-position* in which it is usual to stand before the introductory steps. This is also sometimes known as *extended hold* and is used in the steps around the end of the rink in the Swing Dance. The choice of introductory steps is left to the skaters, but for test purposes they cannot exceed seven steps for either partner.

G. *Hand-in-hand position used as start to dances and during Swing Dance*

For the Dutch Waltz a suggested start would be four steps, starting on the left foot, each step consisting of three counts. The Canasta Tango can be started in a similar way except that the girl would be on the other side of the man. This dance should be started facing one end of the rink and about one third of the way up the rink on the midline. The Swing Dance is started at one corner of the rink facing the length of the ice surface. The girl is on the man's left, and a suggested start is for the girl to skate a left forward inside mohawk, the two edges of which consist of two beats each, and then drop into a left back outside swing roll of four beats. During this time the man skates a right forward outside of two beats, followed by a left forward inside of two beats, and a right forward outside swing roll of four beats. While these steps are being skated, the partners will come into a closed position. These introductory edges form one lobe, the start of which should be aimed diagonally toward the center line of the rink. In place of the mohawk, many ladies prefer to do a right forward outside three, consisting of two beats on the forward outside edge and two beats on the back inside, then dropping onto a four-beat back outside swing roll on the left foot.

157

There are at present twenty dances in the official test schedule of the United States Figure Skating Association, and more may be added in the near future. Descriptions of these dances, as well as more detailed explanation of terms, are contained in the *USFSA Rulebook*. The *Rulebook* may be purchased from the association for $3 by writing to the address given in the Introduction.

A. *Weak posture, slouched shoulders, girl's hip not held firmly*

B. *Bad posture, girl's hand over man's shoulder, man's hand too low*

Errors in Dance Positions

Illustration 69

23. Three Dances

The three dances presented in this section—the Dutch Waltz, the Canasta Tango, and the Swing Dance—are from the Preliminary Dance Test, one of the official tests of the United States Figure Skating Association. The descriptions and the diagrams of these dances are reproduced from the *USFSA Rulebook*. The following abbreviations are used:

R	right	O	outside
L	left	I	inside
F	forward	XS	cross stroke
B	backward	SR	swing roll
		XR	cross roll

The Dutch Waltz

MUSIC: Waltz 3/4

TEMPO: 46 measures of 3 beats per minute

THIS IS A SET-PATTERN DANCE

This is a simple dance for beginners consisting of forward steps only, with partners in Kilian position. The introduction must not contain more than seven steps for either partner. Suggested introductory steps are two straight steps, LF of three beats, and RF of three beats.

The dance starts in one corner of the rink, progressing down the side and across the end, where it repeats down the other side and across the end to the start, thus requiring two sequences of the dance for one round of the rink.

The dance is skated to slow, deliberate waltz music and consists mostly of progressive sequences interspersed with long rolling edges. It thus allows beginners to devote their attention to getting the feel of the music instead of worrying about complicated steps, and allows them to enjoy rhythmical motion in their skating.

159

Upright position, good carriage, and easy flow without too much effort are desired in the dance. The partners should strive for unison of free leg swings and soft knee action throughout the dance.

INVENTOR: George Muller.

FIRST PERFORMED: Broadmoor Ice Palace, Colorado Springs, 1948

Dutch Waltz: Set-pattern Dance
Diagram 18

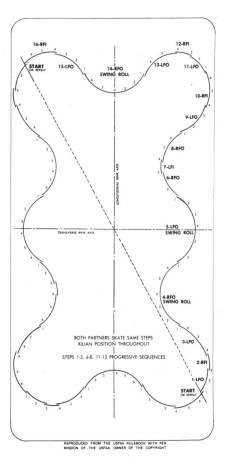

The Canasta Tango

MUSIC: Tango 4/4

TEMPO: 26 measures of 4 beats per minute

THIS IS A SET-PATTERN DANCE

This dance is skated in reverse Kilian position, that is, with the lady on the man's left. It is a very simple dance with a three-fold purpose: first, to introduce the tango rhythm to those at the Preliminary dance level; second, to give the skater experience in the large eight-count half circles, giving him more speed and confidence in his edges; third, to provide more variety for the less experienced dancers.

If the fundamental rules of skating and dancing are observed, there should be no particular difficulty with this dance. The first chassé (Steps 3 and 4) is done with both feet side by side on count 4; be sure to transfer the weight to the right foot, though—do not skate on both feet at the same time. The other chassés marked* are slightly different.

160

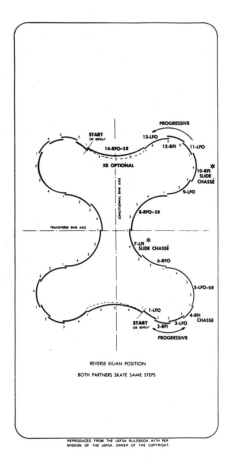

Canasta Tango: Set-pattern Dance
Diagram 19

As the weight is transferred to the new skating foot, the free foot slides off the ice in front of the skater, returning close beside the skating foot just in time for a smooth transition to the next edge. Judicious use of knee action on these edges can do a great deal to help the tango expression. Here, too, is a good place for the beginner to practice extending the free leg as straight as possible, and pointing the toe down, not up! The skater should watch that Steps 9-13 are skated on a good edge so that Step 14 RFO can be aimed somewhat toward the center of the rink and so placed accurately as shown on the diagram. This step (14) may be started, optionally, with a cross stroke in which the right foot crosses in front of the left foot at the end of Step 13 and the push onto the RFO is made from the outside edge of the left foot. [Steps 13 and 14 together form a cross roll. For a description, see Chapter 20.]

An effort should be made to keep the feet fairly close together at the start of the transition, but it is of the utmost importance that a toe push be avoided.

Neat footwork, tango expression, and good carriage should be maintained throughout the dance.

INVENTOR: James B. Francis

FIRST PERFORMED: The University Skating Club, Toronto, 1951

The Swing Dance

MUSIC: Fox-trot 4/4

TEMPO: 24 measures of 4 beats per minute

THIS IS A SET-PATTERN DANCE

This is a dance designed for beginners consisting of the basic edges, forward and backward. It presents a relaxed method of changing from forward to backward skating, requires the man to learn to lead while skating backward as well as forward, makes steps of each skater identical, even though similar steps are not skated at the same time, and makes it possible for two ladies (or two men) to learn to dance or practice it as a couple.

While the diagram shows correct curvature of edges and lobes, such depth of curvature should not be expected from a Preliminary Test dancer. It does, however, present a goal toward which the skater should aim.

The dance may be started at two points in the rink.

The dance as skated down the length of the rink contains four curvatures, or lobes, and is skated in waltz position. The one skating forward during the first set of lobes in the straightaway will be skating backward when these four lobes are skated on the opposite side of the rink.

The chassé sequences apply to both forward and backward skating. First step of the sequence is a normal outside edge of one beat. Second step is an inside edge of one beat stroked sideways, during which the free foot is lifted from the ice and is not allowed to move to a position either in front of or behind the skater, but should be held directly beneath the skater in readiness to accept the skater's weight at the start of the third step. Third step is a normal outside edge of two beats. During the second beat, the skaters must begin a strong change of edge in order to stroke smoothly into the next edge.

162

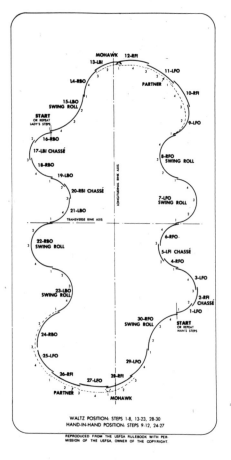

Swing Dance: Set-pattern Dance
Diagram 20

The third and fourth lobes of the straightaway consist of two four-beat swing rolls.

The end sequences consist of seven steps at each end of the rink. Each step of the sequence is held for two full beats except the last step (Steps 15 and 30), which is a swing roll of four beats. Skate the end steps with soft knee action, be relaxed, and try to give the appearance of having fun.

Step 9 or 24. The person skating backward releases his or her left hand and curves his edge away from the partner in order to be in position to step forward on next step.

163

Step 10 or 25. Both skate forward. Skater to the left is the one who has just stepped from backward to forward. Hold nearest hands, but do not crowd each other.

Step 11 or 26. Both still skate forward. Skater to right skates slightly faster than his partner.

Step 12 or 27. Both still skate forward. Skater to the right should now be slightly in advance of skater to left, and should be ready to skate RFI mohawk at the next step. Try to keep facing each other at this time, but don't spoil the relaxed effect.

Step 13 or 28. The person to the right skates a RFI mohawk and finishes the mohawk in front of the partner.

Step 14 or 29. Skater who did the mohawk is now skating backward directly in front of the partner.

Step 15 or 30. Change curvature and skate a four-beat swing roll in waltz position.

The dance positions are waltz position when skating the lengths of the rink and hand-in-hand position at end sequences to allow both skaters to skate forward on Steps 10, 11, 12 or 25, 26, 27. Separate by at least 24 inches and hold arms relaxed. Appearance of arms during end sequences up to Step 14 or 29 is left to discretion of skaters. Assume waltz position in time for Step 15 or 30.

Any type of forward inside mohawk is permissible so long as the balance and control is good and the execution is pleasing to watch.

INVENTOR: Hubert Sprott

FIRST PERFORMED: Broadmoor Ice Palace, Colorado Springs, 1948.

Part V

24. How to Skate a Figure Eight

Now that you have been introduced to free style and ice dancing, it would be a pity to end this book without touching on that branch which gave figure skating its name: the skating of geometrical patterns, of which the figure eight is the simplest form. There are seventy figures in the present USFSA official tests, all based on this fundamental pattern. The majority of these figures contain turns that have not been dealt with in this book. The subject is a vast one and the difficulty when writing a book such as the present one is knowing when to stop. As there are already several books on the market that deal with this subject, only the two basic forward eights will be described here.

164   The idea behind an eight is that you skate a circle on one foot, come back to the place where you started from, and then skate a circle on the other foot, once more returning to your starting point. But this is not enough for the serious figure skater; on clean ice his blade leaves a white mark, and he therefore regards his eight as a drawing to be executed with care and exactitude. Not only does he want his figure eight to be completely symmetrical, the right size, and skated in good form, but, as he repeats the figure, he tries to put each line as nearly on top of the preceding ones as possible.

It has been said earlier that the mark on the ice is called the "trace" or "tracing"; the starting point is known as the *center.* You have already met the term "long axis" in this book, so you will readily understand that in the case of an eight it is an imaginary line running the length of the figure which, if the figure is properly executed, will cut each circle into two equal halves. A second imaginary line, known as the *short axis,* cuts the long axis at right angles, and the center of the figure is located where these two lines intersect. The short axis, therefore, divides one circle from the other. Diagram 21 will help to make all this clear.

165

(In other skating literature you may sometimes meet different names for the long and short axes. For the short axis the alternative names are the *cross, transverse,* or *minor axis,* and the long axis is occasionally referred to as the *major axis.*)

The size of each circle should be such that its diameter is about three times the skater's height, but some latitude is allowed in this, particularly for very tall skaters who may find they are taking up too much space on the rink. A figure is always started from rest and, in tests and competitions, is skated three times without stopping. In the case of a simple eight this would mean that six circles would have been

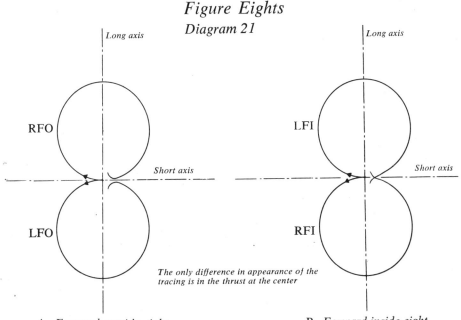

Figure Eights
Diagram 21

Long axis

Long axis

RFO

LFI

Short axis

Short axis

LFO

RFI

The only difference in appearance of the tracing is in the thrust at the center

A. *Forward outside eight*

B. *Forward inside eight*

completed, three on each foot. In practice, you may continue the figure as many times as you wish, but it is essential to move your center to clean ice periodically so that you can see what you are doing. Many beginners continue to go around and around, using the same center, until their tracings form a track about a foot wide. This is ridiculous, as by this time they cannot see what they are doing and the habit encourages untidiness.

If you have laid down a really good figure on the first time around, one of your aims should then be to put the next tracings as nearly on top of the first as possible. This superimposition of one line on the other (often loosely referred to as "tracing" the figure) is officially regarded as of less importance than such other considerations as symmetry and form. However, there is no doubt that in tests and competitions, provided there are no gross errors, accurately superimposed tracings make a very great impression.

There are several ways of moving the arms, shoulders, body, and free leg during an eight, all of which can produce a good result. However, the method to be described here also teaches certain principles of control that you will find helpful in more advanced figures and in movements where it is necessary to move shoulders, hips, and free leg independently.

At first it helps to mark out with the heel of your blade a small cross on the ice to indicate the intersection of the long and short axes, but as soon as possible you should dispense with this. Stand at the center of your figure in the first position for a forward outside edge just as you were shown on page 84, Illustration 31A. As the figure is going to be started on your right forward outside edge, you will stand with your right blade on and along the short axis with your right toe about an inch behind the intersection of the two axes.

Having taken your position, you must now stand still for a moment and think. See the circle you are about to make in your mind's eye and try to judge the farthest point your circle must travel out from the long axis. The farthest point out will be when you have skated a quarter of the circle, so that if your circle is going to be sixteen feet in diameter the first quarter of the circle will be just eight feet out from the long axis. The mapping out of the circle in your mind, particularly the first quarter, is highly important because most beginners go far too far out at the start and then wonder why they cannot get back to their center.

Keep your weight over the left foot and, with the utmost concentration on what you are doing, start your knee bend and strike onto a right outside. Illustration 31B (p. 84) shows the position immediately after the start, except that the skater could have a little more bend of the skating knee. Notice that the head does not turn over the right shoulder, nor does the skating foot twist to the right; all the skater does is to push and lean. You should hold this position without moving a muscle until you have completed the first third of the circle. Later on it is a good idea to hold this first position even longer, but this is early in your figure skating career and we cannot expect miracles. Just to hold the position until the first third is very difficult for a beginner, as he will be battling with swing shortly after the push. When you learned to skate half circles, your change of position was made much earlier, but now the movement has to be distributed over a greater distance. When you arrive at the first third, look down at your right hand: is it still over the tracing or has it wandered inside the curve? Ask a friend to tell you whether your free foot is still in position, with the heel approximately over the tracing, or whether it is swinging outside the curve.

If you have reached the first third satisfactorily, slowly pass your free leg and foot forward but still keep your free hip, shoulder and arm back. If your free hip (in this case your left) comes forward with your left leg, you may never make it back to center. The slow swing forward of the left leg should occupy the whole of the second third of the circle, at the end of which you can carefully allow your shoulders and hips to rotate to a position where they are square to your tracing. At this point try to stop them rotating any further and continue the curve toward your center in this position. From the time your free leg starts its forward movement, you will gradually and almost imperceptibly straighten your skating knee until it is just flexed. Just before you arrive back to center bring both feet together, start the new knee bend, and at the same time rotate your hips and shoulders so that you can thrust onto the left forward outside in a well-controlled first position. Repeat exactly the same movements of the arms, shoulders, and free leg on the left outside. When you have completed the figure three or more times, finish it by simply coming into the center on your left foot; then change feet and skate off the figure along the cross axis.

There are many subtle errors possible in this figure that would take pages of description, so it is only possible to deal with the main ones here. If you find yourself coming in short of your center—that is, making a six instead of an eight—it helps to lift the free side very slightly during the latter part of the circle. This assists in correcting any tendency to press the skating hip into the circle, which, by forcing the blade over onto a sharper edge, may be causing the trouble. Another reason you may come in short of the center is striking onto too shallow an edge at the start and therefore going out much too far in the first part of the circle (Diagram 22A). Yet another fault is just the

168

Errors in Forward Eights *Diagram 22*

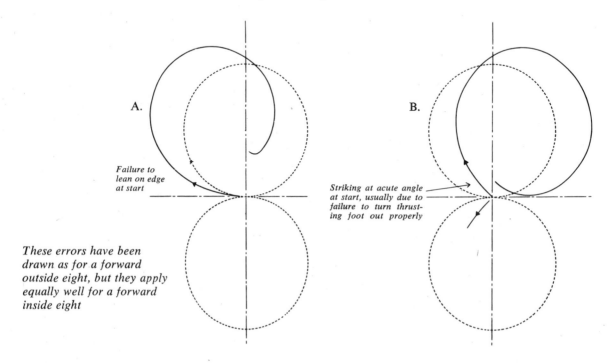

A.

Failure to lean on edge at start

B.

Striking at acute angle at start, usually due to failure to turn thrusting foot out properly

These errors have been drawn as for a forward outside eight, but they apply equally well for a forward inside eight

opposite of the one just described—that is, cutting into the circle at an angle as the strike is made (Diagram 22B). This may be caused by turning the head over the skating shoulder as the thrust is made or by failing to turn the thrusting foot out correctly. Note that the thrust in a figure is directly back, not to the side as in the stroke used around the rink. There must, of course, be no pushing from the toe. In figure skating you can actually fail a test through this fault.

Several types of apparatus in the form of giant compasses have been invented and are extensively used by figure skaters to mark circles on the ice and thereby help them to get their circles the right size and shape. They are used for practice purposes alone and never in tests or competitions; they should be used in practice with caution. They are excellent for *checking* circles once they have been skated or for giving a beginner an idea of what a perfect circle looks like and, therefore, of the picture he must hold in his mind. They can also be used effectively for a skater to discover how a particular turn feels when skated on a true circle, but any skater who thinks that, simply by drawing a circle on the ice and skating around it, he is going to learn to skate a circle, is doomed to disappointment.

In the early days of ice compasses I remember one rink where at the beginning of the season one was used indiscriminately by nearly every figure skater in the club. At the end of three months the ice compass broke and had to be sent for repair. The result was disastrous: there was scarcely a skater who could skate anything resembling a circle—the conception of circle was totally lacking. With the perfect marking already on the ice, there had been no need for them even to think about circle; the only thing they had learned was to follow a line on the ice, and if it wasn't there they had no mental image to fall back on.

You can also try the forward inside eight. The principles as regards the actual tracing on the ice are more or less the same as for the forward outside. The positions at the start and just after the thrust are the same as in Illustration 33A and B, p. 88, but this time try to hold your first position until you reach the half circle, at which point pass your free leg slowly forward and rotate your shoulders gently until the left shoulder and arm are slightly back and the right arm and shoulder forward; then hold this position until you bring your feet together for the new thrust, when you should complete the movement of your arms and shoulders so that you are ready to strike onto the new edge. There should be a slow rise of your skating knee as the free leg passes forward.

170   The commonest fault here is passing the free foot across the curve immediately after the start (see Illustration 23C, p. 69), causing a wild swing that can only be saved by swinging the free foot immediately forward and reversing the arms and shoulders strongly. To control the edge, press your free hip slightly forward immediately after the thrusting foot has left the ice and keep your free foot a little inside the tracing. In this way you should be able to hold your position indefinitely.

In the eights described, as well as in all figures, try to watch and criticize the tracing as you go around. For example, in a forward outside eight, as you pass the long axis half way around on the left foot, try to see how far out you went on your return to center during the preceding circle on the right foot. If you think it is correct, see that you go out an equal distance when returning on your left foot. This is known as *lining up the figure*. On the other hand, if you think your first circle was wrong, skate the correct circle on your left foot and try to correct the circle on the right foot next time around. In tests and competitions it is very important to make such corrections and not just slavishly trace an error.

Glossary and Index

Page references in boldface following an entry indicate detailed discussion in the text or the location of illustrations (illus.) or diagrams (diag.). Figures following the latter abbreviations indicate page numbers, *not* illustration numbers. In definitions, words defined elsewhere in this Glossary are in italics. The following abbreviations are used here or elsewhere in this book, often in combination (RBI, LFO, etc.):

I	inside
O	outside
B	backward, or back
F	forward
R	right
L	left
XR	cross roll
SR	swing roll
USFSA	United States Figure Skating Association

arabesque See *spiral.*

axis 83–85, 165 An imaginary straight line around which skating curves are symmetrically grouped. See *long axis, short axis.*

back 62 When referring to a part of the body, indicates that it is pressing away from the direction in which the *skating* toe is pointing, irrespective of whether the skater is traveling forward or backward.

back inside edge 103–105, illus., diag. The curve made when a skater travels backward, leaning over onto the *inside edge* of the *blade.*

back outside edge 61, 82, illus. 82 The curve made when a skater travels backward, leaning over onto the *outside edge* of the *blade.*

back outside three A turn made on one foot from a curve on a *back outside edge* to another curve on the *forward inside edge.*

barrier 77, illus. 78 The rail or wooden structure (usually three to four feet high) around an ice rink. Also called "the *boards.*"

basic dance movements Various movements dealt with in this book, which make up the elements of *ice dancing.*

basic free style The easier movements in *free style* dealt with in this book. See *free style.*

Basic Test Program 11, 13 A series of graded tests sponsored by the USFSA and designed specifically for beginners.

blade 24–28, illus. 24, 25 The vertical section of a metal *skate.* The bottom of the blade is hollow ground to form two sharp *edges.*

boards See *barrier.*

bunny hop 111–112, illus. A simple jump in which the skater travels straight forward on one foot, jumps onto the *toe*

171

pick of the other, and pushes straight forward onto the flat of the *blade* of the starting foot.

Canasta Tango 160–161, diag.   A simple *ice dance* to tango rhythm.

center 165   The point where the *long* and *short axes* intersect, forming the starting and finishing point of a *figure*.

center (a spin) 128   To keep a spin rotating on a fixed point on the ice. See also *travel*.

172

change of edge 106–107, illus., diag. Rocking over on one foot from one edge to its opposite, forming a *serpentine* pattern on the ice.

chassé 141, 145–146, 148   In *ice dancing*, a step starting on an *outside edge* in which the *free* foot is brought beside and level with the *skating* foot and is placed onto an *inside edge* while the *skating* foot is lifted vertically and very slightly off the ice. See also *slide chassé*.

chassé sequence 141–142, 148–149, illus. 141, 148   A chassé followed by a strike onto the original *outside edge*.

check   A movement of a part or parts of the body to counteract and thereby control the natural rotation, or *swing*, set up by a turn, or *edge*.

cherry flip   See *toe loop jump*.

closed 74–75, illus.   Describes position in which a part or parts of the *free* side of the body press toward the direction in which the *skating* toe is pointing.

closed mohawk 154–155, illus. 153   A *mohawk* in which the instep of the *free* foot is brought to the heel of the *skating* foot, and, as the change in feet takes place, the *free* foot and leg pass across and in front of the *skating* leg.

closed position   In *ice dancing*, a position in which the man and lady face each other. Also known as *waltz position*.

cross axis   See *short axis*.

cross ground 25, illus.   Denoting a *blade* sharpened by a grinding wheel rotating across the width of the *blade*.

crossover 71–73, 100–102, illus. 71–73, 101   A movement started on an *outside* *edge*, forward or backward, in which the *free* foot passes around and in front of the *skating* toe and is placed onto an *inside edge*. See also *run*.

cross roll (forward) 146–147, illus., diag. A movement starting on a *forward outside edge* in which the *free* foot is passed around and in front of the *skating* toe onto a *forward outside edge*, with a *thrust* from the original *outside edge*.

cross stroke   A term used mainly in *ice dancing*, a step started with the feet crossed in which impetus is gained from the *outside edge* of the foot which is about to become the *free* foot. Both *crossovers* and *cross rolls* involve *cross strokes*.

dance steps   In *free style*, synonymous with *footwork*, denoting a sequence of *edges*, often containing complex turns, usually skated to music and forming a link between jumps, spins, and other movements in a *free style* program.

deepen (an edge)   When skating an *edge*, to cause the curvature to increase (that is, to decrease the radius of the curve).

drop mohawk 92–93, 113–115, illus. 92, 93   A *mohawk* followed by a change of feet, the whole movement continuing in the curve of the original *edge*.

Dutch roll 147   An older term for a *cross roll*.

Dutch Waltz 158–159, diag.   A simple *ice dance* consisting of *forward edges*.

edge 25, 61–62   (1) One of the two sharp sides of the *blade* of a *skate*. (2) The curve resulting when a skater leans in such a way as to cause one of these *edges* to cut into the ice.

eight 164–170, diag. 165, 168   A simple skating *figure* consisting of two circles, each of a diameter about three times the skater's height, starting and finishing at a specific point on the ice. In tests, an *eight* is started from a standstill and three circles are skated on each foot without pause.

employed   See *skating*.

extended hold   See *hand-in-hand position*.

Also, an imaginary line around which consecutive half circles are grouped. Also called *major axis*.

loop jump 132–134, illus., diag. A jump in which the skater takes off from a *back outside edge,* makes one turn in the air, and lands on the original *back outside edge.*

major axis See *long axis*.

master tooth The lowest and most important spike in the group of saw-toothed projections at the front of a figure *blade*. Also called "master pick."

matched set 26 A combination of skating boot and *skate* in which the *skate* has been fixed to the boot at the factory. See *mounting*.

mazurka 121–122, illus. A simple skating jump taken from a *back edge* in which the skater strikes his *free* toe into the ice, executes a half turn in the air, lands on the toe of the other foot, and pushes onto a *forward edge* of the opposite foot.

minor axis See *short axis*.

mohawk 79–82, 92–93, 113–115, 150, 152–155, illus. 80–81, 92, 93, 151, 153 A turn from forward to backward (or backward to forward), from one foot to the other.

mounting 26–27 The fixing of a *skate* to a boot. This must be done with great precision so that the *skate* is aligned with the natural run of the foot: not obliquely to the natural run nor too far to the inside or outside.

natural rotation The normal direction of rotation of a skater's body set up by the curve of an *edge*. *Edges* traveling in a clockwise direction tend to rotate the body clockwise around its axis, and vice versa.

neutral (position) 64, illus. 65 A position in which arms and shoulders, or hips, are square to the line of travel of the skater.

one-foot snowplow 38, illus. A skating stop in which one foot is placed on the ice ahead of the body and broadside to the direction of travel.

one-foot spin 126–129, illus., diag. 127 A skating spin executed on one foot.

open 74–75, illus. A position in which a part or parts of the *free* side of the body press away from the direction in which the *skating* toe is pointing.

open mohawk 79–82, illus. 80–81 A *mohawk* in which the heel of the *free* foot is brought into a position opposite the instep of the *skating* foot before the turn. After the change of feet has taken place, the *free* leg finishes behind the heel of the *skating* foot in an *open* position.

optional pattern dance A dance which, under certain circumstances, may be skated to various patterns while still preserving the correct edges.

outside edge 25, 61, 65–70, 82, 83–87, 94–99, illus., diag. 25, 66–67, 82, 84, 86, 95, 98, 99 The *edge* of the *skating blade* farthest away from the midline of the body, or the curve skated on this *edge*.

pair skating 11 A branch of *figure skating* involving various combined lifts, spins, and *free style* movements executed simultaneously and in harmony by two skaters.

pattern In *ice dancing,* the design in which the *edges* and steps of an *ice dance* are laid out on the ice.

pick 24–25, illus. One of the sharp projections at the front of a figure *skate,* used to grip the ice in certain jumps and spins. Also known as a "toe pick," "toe rake," or "tooth."

pivot 119–120, 129–130, 134, illus. 129, 134 A movement in *free style* in which the skater places a *toe pick* in the ice and circles around it.

prepared position The correct position of the body immediately before a turn, *change of edge,* etc.

progressive 142–144, 149–150, illus. 143, 149 In *ice dancing,* a step, almost invariably started on an *outside edge,* in which a change of feet takes place by the *free* foot passing the *skating* foot and being placed on the ice on an *inside edge.* Also known as a *run,* particularly in Great Britain and Canada.

progressive sequence A *progressive* followed by a strike onto a third *edge*, generally the original *outside edge*.

push See *thrust*.

racing skate See *speed skate*.

radius 26 The front-to-back curve of a *figure blade*.

rake See *pick*.

reverse Kilian position See *Kilian position reversed*.

rocker (1) An advanced skating turn, not dealt with in this book. (2) Same as *radius*.

Rocker Fox-trot 155 A dance contained in the Silver Test of the USFSA test structure.

roll 86–87, 106, 139–141, 146–147, illus., diag. 84, 86, 147 An *edge* usually consisting of one-third to half a circle which curves in the opposite direction to the preceding *edge* on the other foot.

run 71 (1) See *progressive*. (2) A succession of *crossovers* used to get up speed for a jump, etc.

salchow 122–125, illus., diag. A jump consisting of a turn in the air from a *back inside edge* of one foot to a *back outside edge* on the other. Named for Ulrich Salchow, a former world champion.

scissor (jump) 122, illus. Sometimes known as "scissors," a jump involving a half turn from backward to forward. When started on an RBO the left *toe pick* is struck into the ice to assist the jump and the right leg crosses *behind* the left in the air.

scratch spin See *toe spin*.

sculling 49, illus. A method of two-footed progression forward or backward by an in-and-out movement of the feet.

serpentine See *change of edge*.

set To fix a blade in a specific position on a boot. See *mounting*.

set-pattern dance A dance which lends itself easily to being so laid out in its design that certain steps are always taken at specific places on the ice surface. See *optional pattern*.

sharpening See *grinding*.

short axis 165 In *figure skating*, an imaginary straight line dividing one circle from the other and at right angles to the *long axis;* also called *cross axis, minor axis,* or *transverse axis*. See also *long axis*.

Silver Tango 155 An *ice dance* contained in the Silver Test of the USFSA test structure.

skate A metal runner used for progression over the ice, often used loosely to refer to the combination of boot and *skate*.

skating 62, illus. 61 Describes the side of the body or any part thereof on the same side as the foot on which a skater happens to be at any particular moment.

slide chassé 145–146, illus. 144–145 In *ice dancing*, a step starting on a *forward outside edge* in which the *free* foot is brought close beside the *skating* foot, placed onto a *forward inside edge,* and the original *skating* foot is extended forward.

snowplow stop 37–38, illus. A two-footed movement in which both toes are turned in, causing the *blades* to skid, thus bringing the skater to a stop.

speed skate A *skate* particularly adapted for racing. The *blade* is thin, has no curve from front to back, and extends some distance in front of the toe of the boot.

spiral 112, 120, illus. A position in *free style* roughly comparable to an arabesque in ballet. The name is taken from the pattern formed on the ice when the position is held for an extended period.

spiral take-off 105, diag. A method of thrusting from a *back inside edge* on one foot to a *back inside edge* on the other. See *sculling*, which is similar in appearance.

spread-eagle mohawk 81 A *mohawk* in which, just before the turn, the *free* foot is turned out and placed on the ice in line with the *skating* foot just before the turn instead of being brought close and into position approximately at right angles to the *skating* foot. Now considered old-fashioned and sloppy.

stanchion illus. 24 One of the two main supporting sections of a *skate*, connecting the *blade* to the sole or heel plate.

Basic Ice Skating Skills

176

strike (1) The action of transferring the weight from the thrusting foot onto the new *skating* foot. (2) The mark or point on the ice at which such a transference is made.

stroke The method of propulsion over the ice, coordinating *thrust,* knee bend, and transference of weight.

superimposition 166 When skating *figures,* the placing of one tracing as nearly as possible on top of a preceding one.

swing 66 (1) A passing of the *free* leg past the *skating* leg. (2) The rotation, particularly if uncontrolled, of the body or parts of the body, set up by a curve of an *edge* or movement of a turn.

Swing Dance 161–163, diag. A simple *ice dance* in 4/4 rhythm.

swing mohawk 81 Any *mohawk* in which the *free* foot is swung past the *skating* foot before being brought back into position to make the turn.

swing roll 139–141 In *ice dancing,* an *edge* held for several beats during which the *free* leg is swung past the *skating* leg before being returned into position prior to the new *strike.*

T stop 56–58, illus. 57 A stop in which the *free* foot is placed on the ice behind and at right angles to the *skating* foot, thus producing a skid and bringing the skater to a stop.

take-off (1) The action of leaving the ice in a jump. (2) In *figures,* the *thrust* from one foot to the other at the start of or during a *figure.*

tap loop jump See *toe loop jump.*

three turn 75–79, illus. A turn on one foot from forward to backward or backward to forward, from an *outside* to an *inside edge* or an *inside* to an *outside edge,* the *edges* before and after the turn being on the same circle. During the turn the *skating* foot rotates in the natural direction of the *edge.* Also often called simply a "three."

thrust A means of starting from rest or gaining speed while in motion by pushing against the ice with the *blade* of the *skate.* When starting a right *forward outside edge* from rest, the *thrust* is made from the *inside edge* of the left *blade.*

toe loop jump 118–119, illus. A jump in which the skater takes off from a *back outside edge,* strikes the toe of the *free* foot into the ice, and makes one turn in the air, landing on the original *back outside edge.* Also called *cherry flip* or *tap loop jump.*

toe pick See *pick.*

toe spin 126–129, illus., diag. A spin executed on the lowest *toe pick* of the *blade.* Same as *scratch spin.*

tooth See *pick.*

trace When skating *figures,* usually used in the sense of "to superimpose." See *superimposition.*

tracing The white mark made on the ice by the *blade* of a *skate.*

transverse axis See *short axis.*

travel 128, diag. 127 In spinning, to move across the ice while rotating. See *center (a spin).*

tucking 142, 144 In *ice dancing,* the slight cross behind of the back foot on the second step of a forward *progressive.* The movement is still controversial in some quarters.

unemployed See *free.*

waltz jump 114–117, illus. A jump in which the skater takes off from a *forward outside edge,* executes a half turn in the air (turning in the direction of a *forward outside three*), and lands on the *back outside edge* on the other foot. Also known as a "three jump," particularly in Canada and Great Britain.

waltz position See *closed position.*

waltz three 89–91, illus., diag., 90, 91 A *three turn* from a *forward outside edge* followed by a change of feet, the whole movement continuing in the curve of the original *edge.*